PURSUING
COMMON VALUES
OF HUMANITY
CHINA'S APPROACH TO DEMOCRACY,
FREEDOM AND HUMAN RIGHTS

全人类共同价值的追求与探索

民主自由人权的中国实践

新华社中国民主自由人权观课题组　编著

新华出版社

图书在版编目（CIP）数据

全人类共同价值的追求与探索：民主自由人权的中国实践 / 新华社中国民主自由人权观课题组编著.
北京：新华出版社,2021.11（2025.2重印）
ISBN 978-7-5166-6113-0

Ⅰ.①全… Ⅱ.①新… Ⅲ.①社会主义民主–研究–中国 ②自由–研究–中国 ③人权–研究–中国 Ⅳ.①D621

中国版本图书馆CIP数据核字（2021）第221947号

全人类共同价值的追求与探索：民主自由人权的中国实践

编　　著：	新华社中国民主自由人权观课题组		
出 版 人：	匡乐成	选题统筹：	许　新
责任编辑：	张　谦	封面设计：	今亮后声

出版发行：新华出版社
地　　址：北京石景山区京原路8号　　邮　　编：100040
网　　址：http://www.xinhuapub.com
经　　销：新华书店、新华出版社天猫旗舰店、京东旗舰店及各大网店
购书热线：010－63077122　　中国新闻书店购书热线：010－63072012

照　　排：六合方圆
印　　刷：大厂回族自治县众邦印务有限公司
成品尺寸：170mm×240mm
印　　张：12　　字　　数：100千字
版　　次：2021年12月第一版　　印　　次：2025年2月第二次印刷
书　　号：ISBN 978-7-5166-6113-0
定　　价：48.00元

版权专有，侵权必究。如有质量问题，请与出版社联系调换：010-63077124

各国历史、文化、制度、发展水平不尽相同，但各国人民都追求和平、发展、公平、正义、民主、自由的全人类共同价值。[1]

　　和平与发展是我们的共同事业，公平正义是我们的共同理想，民主自由是我们的共同追求。[2]

——习近平

---

[1] 习近平在中国共产党与世界政党领导人峰会上的主旨讲话，2021年7月6日
[2] 习近平在中华人民共和国恢复联合国合法席位50周年纪念会议上的讲话，2021年10月25日

导　言 / 001

第一章　人民当家作主：追求民主价值的大逻辑 / 004
  1.1　历史逻辑：人民的选择 / 006
  1.2　理论逻辑：人民的作品 / 010
  1.3　实践逻辑：主动的建构 / 012
  1.4　价值逻辑：让人民自由 / 018

第二章　全过程人民民主：落实人民主权的新形态 / 021
  2.1　"人"是怎么选的？/ 022
  2.2　"事"是怎么议的？/ 024
  2.3　"策"是怎么定的？/ 026
  2.4　"权"是怎么用的？/ 028

第三章　管用的民主：判断制度成色的试金石 / 032
  3.1　致善政的"治理型民主" / 033
  3.2　有活力的"效率型民主" / 036
  3.3　汇众智的"动力型民主" / 037
  3.4　可检验的"系统性民主" / 040

第四章　实践智慧：追求全人类共同价值的启示 / 043
　　4.1　"致治"之道：三个"关键应用" / 044
　　4.2　实现全人类共同价值："四项原则" / 051
　　4.3　"时代之问"：中国方案 / 055

结　语 / 059

编写说明与致谢 / 060

附　录 / 070

Contents

Introduction / 089

Chapter I The Running of the Country by the People: The Overarching Logic of Pursuing the Value of Democracy / 093

    1.1 Logic of History: The People's Choice / 096

    1.2 Theoretical Logic: The Work of the People / 103

    1.3 Logic in Practice: Initiative in Institutional Design / 106

    1.4 Logic in values: Emancipating the People / 116

Chapter II Whole-process Democracy: a New Form of Implementing People's Sovereignty / 121

    2.1 How Does China Select Officials? / 122

    2.2 How do People Participate in Public Affairs Deliberations? / 126

    2.3 How are Policies Made? / 129

    2.4 How is "Power" Exercised? / 133

Chapter III A Democracy that Works: a Touchstone for Testing Institutional Effectiveness / 138

    3.1 "Governance Democracy" for Good Governance / 139

    3.2 "Efficient Democracy" with Vitality / 143

    3.3 "Democracy as Driving Force" with Collective Wisdom / 145

    3.4 Testable "Systematic Democracy" / 149

Chapter IV The Wisdom of Practice: The Enlightenment of Pursuing Common Values of Humanity / 154

    4.1 Approach to Sound Governance: Three Leading Features / 156

    4.2 Realizing the Common Values of Humanity: "Four Principles" / 166

    4.3 "Questions of the Times": China's Solution / 172

Conclusion / 178

Editor's Note and Acknowledgments / 180

导 言

新中国成立以来,在世界上人口最多、有56个民族的国家,中国共产党领导人民创造了世所罕见的经济快速发展奇迹和社会长期稳定奇迹。理解这"两大奇迹",既需要深入观察让中国融入世界的改革开放背后的经济逻辑,也需要深入理解追求全人类共同价值过程中,当代中国在民主、自由、人权领域不断探索实践的政治逻辑。

长期以来,外界往往习惯于西方建构的民主逻辑,以"竞争选举""多党轮替""三权鼎立"作为判断一个国家是否民主的首要指标。按照这个评判标准,无法解释中国为何能创造"两大奇迹"。

中国人追求全人类共同价值的长期实践得出的结论是,从人民的视角出发,民主治理的好坏只有一个标准:老百姓能够

全人类共同价值的追求与探索 —— 民主自由人权的中国实践

享受和平发展的红利，过上安宁祥和的幸福生活。现代国家治理的本质在于民主治理。良好的民主，能使自由和人权得到保障和发展。

最早出现在古希腊的"民主"一词，本意为"人民的统治"。而"人民当家作主"在中国正变成越来越生动饱满的现实。

随着时间的推移，衡量民主的西方中心主义标尺已经过时。

中国立足自身实际，探索民主价值实现的守正创新之路，追求人民当家作主的"实质民主"，是全链条、全方位、全覆盖的"全过程人民民主"，致善政的"治理型民主"，有活力的"效率型民主"，汇众智的"动力型民主"，可检验的"系统性民主"，归根到底，是最广泛、最真实、最管用的社会主义民主。

中国在落实人民当家作主的实践中，取得了显著的治理成效，具有高"治商"。解码中国民主的"致治"之道，或可将先进政党、人民至上、聚焦发展喻为三大"关键应用"。

中国是民主自由人权理念"忠实的实践者"和"实践的创新者"，虽仍在路上，但中国的探索追求，已为实现全人类共同价值提供了可以借鉴的重要原则：实践原则——民主的有效性必须通过能否解决绝大多数人实际问题的实践来检验和完善；自主原则——民主自由人权的路径选择必须基于本国国情，外部强加的所谓"民主改造"贻害无穷；时序原则——促进民主、维护自由、保障人权需要循序渐进，不能超越社会发展阶段搞狂飙突进；过程原则——民主自由人权的追求止于至善，没有最好，只有更好。

以"人民当家作主"为本质，以"全过程人民民主"为特征，以是否符合国情、是否有效管用、是否得到人民拥护为标准，中国不断提升民主治理水平，使人民的自由、权利和福祉不断增加。中国特色社会主义民主，彰显出一种新型政治文明形态。

第一章

人民当家作主：追求民主价值的大逻辑

中国特色社会主义民主是个新事物，也是个好事物。[1]

——习近平

---

[1] 习近平在庆祝全国人民代表大会成立六十周年大会上的讲话，2014 年 9 月 5 日

假如近 200 年前以撰写《论美国的民主》而知名的托克维尔来到今天的中国，会怎样观察思考这里的故事？

14 亿多人口的国家彻底摆脱了绝对贫困，正在追求逐步实现全体人民共同富裕的奋斗目标；

全世界最大的社会保障网络，覆盖几乎每个中国人的基本医疗、养老保险；

世界第二大经济体，第一大贸易国，每年对世界经济增长的贡献率超过 30%；

全球 50% 的新能源汽车奔驰在全世界里程最长的高速公路网上；全世界里程最长的高铁；全球最便捷的快递网络，遍布城市乡村角落；

10 亿多网民无时无刻不在网络上发布和分享信息；每年毕业大学生数量在世界各国最多；

每天，有 1.6 万户企业在这里诞生，120 多家新的外商企业赶来这个世界最大消费市场和第一大投资目的地；

每年，1 亿多中国人走出国门，到访世界各地，并平安返回；[1]

486.4 万个基层党组织，9500 多万中国共产党党员，[2] 活

---

[1] 以上部分数据摘自中国驻美大使秦刚在卡特中心和乔治·布什美中关系基金会联合举办的对话会上的演讲，中国驻美国大使馆官网，2021 年 9 月 22 日，http://www.china-embassy.org/dshd/202109/t20210923_9594567.htm

[2] 中国共产党党内统计公报，新华网，2021 年 6 月 30 日

跃在960多万平方公里土地上；

……

制度稳则国家稳，制度强则国家强。透过中国取得长期安全、稳定、增长、发展的治理成就，可以得出这样的认知：一种蓬勃发展的民主——中国特色社会主义民主，已经具体而现实地变成了造福14亿多人民的实践。这条民主道路，顺应历史、理论、实践和价值逻辑，坚守全人类共同价值，又立足中国大地实现了创新性发展。

1.1 历史逻辑：人民的选择

人民当家作主的民主道路，是中国人民在历史中的选择。

——民主来路

2021年，一部热播电视剧《觉醒年代》，将中国人拉回100多年前的历史现场：面对列强入侵、国家贫弱、人民困苦的悲惨现实，中国的先进知识分子发起新文化运动，呼吁请来"德先生"和"赛先生"即民主与科学，来救中国；1921年，中国共产党应运而生。这个为劳苦大众奋斗的党，把民主写在大旗上，带领人民取得新民主主义革命胜利，其标志就是1949年中华人民共和国的诞生，实现了中国从几千年封建专制政治向人民民主的伟大飞跃。[1]

上述事实揭示了中国共产党和中国人民选择的民主之路：政党领导人民建立新国家，实现人民当家作主，开启国家现代化进程。理解这一模式首先要读懂中国共产党。它是一个"使命型政党"，把为人民谋幸福、为民族谋复兴作为初心使命。它是"人民的政党"，为人民而生，因人民而兴，在带领和依靠人民闹革命建立新中国的奋斗中，成为人民信任的先锋队和领导核心。

100年前，中国共产党创立，目标就是改变中国国困民穷之面貌，为人民谋幸福，为民族谋复兴。100年来，这一初心未曾改变，这一使命始终在肩。

过去8年，中国共产党领导人民打赢脱贫攻坚战，近1亿农村贫困人口脱离绝对贫困。为实现这一艰巨任务，全国累计选派25.5万个驻村工作队、300多万名第一书记和驻村干部奋战在扶贫战场，1800多名同志殉职。[2]

中国共产党的合法性源自历史，是人心向背决定的，是人民的选择。中国共产党深知这一地位绝非高枕无忧，因而反复告诫全党：密切联系群众是"最大优势"，而脱离群众是"最大危险"。

---

[1]《中共中央关于党的百年奋斗重大成就和历史经验的决议》，2021年11月11日中国共产党第十九届中央委员会第六次全体会议通过

[2] 数据出自"习近平在全国脱贫攻坚总结表彰大会上的讲话"，2021年2月25日

全人类共同价值的追求与探索 — 民主自由人权的中国实践

中共党员干部献身抗疫、脱贫

近400名党员、干部
为抗击新冠肺炎疫情献出了宝贵生命

脱贫攻坚战中
1800多名党员、干部
将生命定格在脱贫攻坚征程上

资料来源：2021年8月发布的《中国共产党的历史使命与行动价值》

——跳出"历史周期率"

历史上王朝更替，"其兴也勃焉""其亡也忽焉"[1]，形成历史周期率。1945年，在延安的窑洞里，毛泽东回答来访的民主人士：我们已经找到新路，我们能跳出这周期率。这条新路，就是民主。[2]

关键问题是，什么样的民主？在政体选择上，近代中国尝试过君主立宪制、议会制、多党制、总统制等多种制度模式，但都以失败告终。1949年9月，新中国成立在即，中国人民政治协商会议第一届全体会议就新国家的政体达成共识：国家最高政权机关为全国人民代表大会。全国人民代表大会闭会期间，

---

[1] 出自《左传·庄公十一年》
[2] 《为中华民族伟大复兴筑牢民主基石——以习近平同志为核心的党中央发展全过程人民民主述评》，新华网，2021年10月12日，http://www.news.cn/2021-10/12/c_1127948849.htm

第一章　人民当家作主：追求民主价值的大逻辑

中央人民政府为行使国家政权的最高机关。各级政权机关一律实行民主集中制。[1]1954年，新中国第一届全国人民代表大会第一次会议召开，通过首部宪法，以人民代表大会制度为根本政治制度的国家治理体系由此确立。

"人民代表大会制度，坚持国家一切权力属于人民，最大限度保障人民当家作主，把党的领导、人民当家作主、依法治国有机结合起来，有效保证国家治理跳出治乱兴衰的历史周期率。"回顾人民代表大会制度走过的67年，中国领导人习近平这样说。[2]

专栏：中国的人民代表大会

中国宪法规定，国家一切权力属于人民。人民既有选举权，又有依法广泛参与国家治理的权利。在中国，人民行使国家权力的机关是全国人民代表大会和地方各级人民代表大会，全国人民代表大会是最高国家权力机关。中国的全国人民代表大会是世界最有影响的议会组织"各国议会联盟"（Inter-Parliamentary Union）的成员。

与此同时，人民代表大会与西方国家的议会也有很大的不同。比如，不同于西方议会，人民代表大会中没有议会党团，

---

[1]《中华人民共和国简史》，人民出版社、当代中国出版社，2021年，第6页
[2] 习近平在中央人大工作会议上发表重要讲话，新华网，2021年10月14日

也不按党派分配席位。人大代表,无论是共产党员,还是民主党派成员或者无党派人士,肩负的都是人民的重托,都是为人民依法履行职责。

中国县乡两级人大代表实行直接选举,县级以上是间接选举。人民可以选举出他们的代表参政议政,并选出国家机关领导人员。人大代表密切联系群众,所有重大立法决策都是依照程序,经过民主酝酿,通过科学决策、民主决策产生。

在全国人大的实践中,很少会否决一项决议,也许有人会因此认为人大不那么重要。但事实是,在进行投票表决之前会进行非常透彻的讨论,好的建议都会被采纳。最终,当代表们进入人民大会堂投票时,他们的关切和意见往往已被考虑和吸收,大家对提交表决的相关文件感到更加满意。当然反对票和弃权票总会有,这也正常。

资料来源:中国人大网,以及秦刚、傅莹关于人大制度的介绍

1.2 理论逻辑:人民的作品

1954年6月新中国第一部宪法的草案公布后,全国约四分之一人口即1.5亿人参加了讨论,提出118万多条意见。[1] 这部

---

[1] 资料出自浙江杭州"五四宪法"历史资料陈列馆

获得全票通过的宪法被称为"人民的宪法"——国家"一切权力属于人民",国号中有"人民",国家权力机关是"人民代表大会",各级政府是"人民政府"……以"人民"之名定义国家制度,意味着人民居于道义制高点,政权必须对人民负责。

——从民主的真谛出发

近代西方资产阶级革命打出自由、民主等口号,激动人心,但实现的只是少数人的民主。直到19世纪中叶轰轰烈烈的工人运动兴起,经过劳苦大众的奋斗,以追求平等与公正为核心的大众民主,才逐渐变成席卷世界的现代潮流,成为全人类共同价值。[1] "人民当家作主"的中国民主实践,是这个世界潮流的一部分。

以追求者姿态踏上民主道路的新中国,力图从现代民主价值来思考和把握本国的民主路径,即马克思所揭示的民主逻辑:国家制度是人的自由产物,人民不是国家的作品,相反,国家是"人民自己的作品",人民成为国家的主人,国家的意义在于最大限度地实现人民自由而全面的发展。[2]

新中国民主实践的社会主义取向,意味着它是资产阶级民

---

[1] 杨光斌:《民主的社会主义之维——兼评资产阶级与民主政治的神话》,《中国社会科学》,2009年第3期

[2] 林尚立:《人民、政党与国家:人民民主发展的政治学分析》,《复旦学报(社会科学版)》,2011年第5期

主的批判者和超越者，所要实现的人民主权，即"人民当家作主"，以人为本，是一种广泛、真实、管用的民主，是"人本"的，而不是"资本"的民主。

——在中国扎根

马克思主义中国化——把马克思主义基本原理同中国具体实际相结合、同中华优秀传统文化相结合，是中国共产党带领人民迎来从站起来、富起来到强起来的理论密码。同样，民主在中国土地上深深扎根，才有蓬勃的生命力。中国的民主发展结合"目标导向"——实现人民幸福、国家富强和民族复兴，"现实国情"——世界上人口最多的发展中国家，以及"历史维度"——五千年文明古国的历史文化传承，不忘本来，吸收外来，面向未来，不断融合、总结、提炼、升华，探索形成了新的民主形态。

在长期的社会主义实践中，中国深刻认识到"贫穷不是社会主义"，也深刻认识到"人民民主是社会主义的生命"。

1.3 实践逻辑：主动的建构

山西普通的农村妇女申纪兰，见证了人民代表大会制度在中国的诞生。1954年9月，25岁的她骑着毛驴走出大山，再转乘汽车、火车到北京，作为民主选举产生的全国人大代表，参加第一届全国人大第一次会议。她在合作社带领姐妹们争取到与男人同工同酬的权利。在她参与投票通过的新中国第一部宪法中,明确规定"中华人民共和国妇女在政治的、经济的、文化的、社会的和家庭的生活各方面享有同男子平等的权利"。2020年6月,91岁的申纪兰辞世。这个当年不识字的农妇,成为连续十三届的全国人大代表,一辈子为人民代言。她的故事,反映了人民代表大会制度设计的特点。

保障妇女参政议政权

资料来源:2019年9月发布的《为人民谋幸福:新中国人权事业发展70年》白皮书

——广泛的代表性

人民代表大会制度,落实的是国家"一切权力属于人民"的宪法原则。民众选举出能够表达自己意愿和利益的代表,组成各级国家权力机关。其中,全国人民代表大会是最高国家权力机关。

全人类共同价值的追求与探索 —— 民主自由人权的中国实践

广泛代表性是这一制度的鲜明特点。目前,中国各级人大代表有262万多人,在地域、行业、民族等结构上与整个社会的人民结构具有整体的对应性,确保国家权力机关能够全面地反映人民意愿。本届全国人大代表中,工人、农民代表占总数的15.7%,55个少数民族均有本民族代表。[1]

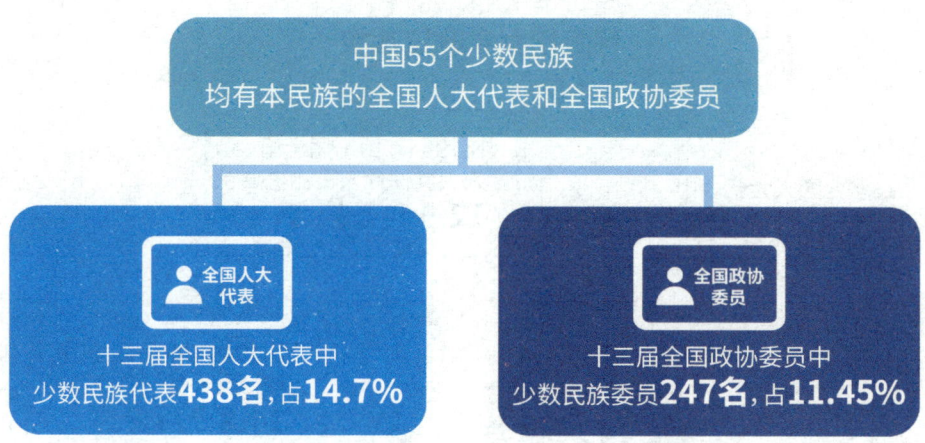

资料来源:2021年6月发布的《中国共产党尊重和保障人权的伟大实践》白皮书

中国的人大代表不脱离各自的生产和工作[2],他们来自各行各业,许多来自基层。这样做的道理是,人民代表身在群众中间,更有利于发挥桥梁纽带作用,使立法更好地接地气、察民情、

---

[1] 国务院新闻办公室:《中国共产党尊重和保障人权的伟大实践》白皮书,2021年6月
[2] 《中华人民共和国全国人民代表大会和地方各级人民代表大会代表法》,中国人大网

聚民智、惠民生。

如果说申纪兰的故事是旧社会翻身农民的民主、女性权利的胜利，"快递小哥"柴闪闪则反映着中国民主与时俱进。作为中国新兴的快递行业数百万快递员群体的代表，柴闪闪2018年当选为全国人大代表。2021年全国人大会议上，柴闪闪代表带来完善网约车、快递、外卖配送等灵活就业劳动者社会保障等多项建议，直接推动了相关法律制度出台。

——民主集中制

中国宪法明确指出，中华人民共和国的国家机构实行民主集中制的原则。全国人民代表大会和地方各级人民代表大会都由民主选举产生，对人民负责，受人民监督。国家行政机关、监察机关、审判机关、检察机关都由人民代表大会产生，对它负责，受它监督。[1] 在党的领导下，各国家机关是一个统一整体，既合理分工，又密切协作，既充分发扬民主，又有效进行集中，克服了议而不决、决而不行、行而不实等不良现象。[2]

民主集中制是原则，也是一种方法——在充分发扬民主基础上形成正确决策并有力地贯彻执行。正因如此，人民代表大会制度形成了治国理政的强大合力，可以切实防止出现相互掣

---

[1]《中华人民共和国宪法》，人民出版社，2018年，第8页
[2] 习近平：《论坚持人民当家作主》，中央文献出版社，2021年，第277页

肘、内耗严重的现象，为中国共产党领导人民创造经济快速发展奇迹和社会长期稳定奇迹提供了重要制度保障。

经过长期实践，中国领导人得出结论：人民代表大会制度是"人类政治制度史上的伟大创造，是在我国政治发展史乃至世界政治发展史上具有重大意义的全新政治制度"。[1]

——三者有机统一

中国共产党不仅完成了建立人民共和国的建国使命，也在执政后解决了民主运行的"超大规模难题"：如何使亿万人民能够成为一个整体，从而把国家权力切实掌握在人民手中？

中国在实践探索中找到答案——"三者有机统一"原则，即坚持党的领导、人民当家作主、依法治国有机统一。党的领导回答了"谁来凝聚人民"，人民当家作主回答了"民主的目标为何"，依法治国回答了"如何治理国家"。

其内在机理是：人民通过中国共产党领导凝聚为有机整体；党和人民共同意志体现并成为宪法和法律；国家以宪法为根本法得以组织、运行和发展；权力运行必须在法治的框架内；人民以中国共产党为核心，通过各种途径和形式依法管理国家事务、管理经济和文化事业、管理社会事务，宪法、法律及其实施都要有效体现人民意志、保障人民权益、激发人民创造力。

---

[1] 习近平在中央人大工作会议上发表重要讲话，新华网，2021年10月14日

——人民当家作主制度体系

新中国的民主制度设计蕴含着防止乱象的深谋远虑：以中国共产党领导的多党合作和政治协商制度，加强社会各种力量的合作协调，防止"党争纷沓、相互倾轧"现象；以民族区域自治制度，铸牢中华民族共同体意识，防止"民族隔阂、民族冲突"现象；以基层群众自治制度，保障人民依法直接行使民主权利，防止"人民形式上有权、实际上无权"现象。

这三项"基本政治制度"与作为"根本政治制度"的人民代表大会制度一起，支撑起人民当家作主制度体系。

——"双轮驱动"：选举+协商

有人形容，中国的民主是"双轮驱动"：既有选举民主——人民通过选举、投票行使权利，又有协商民主——人民内部各方面在重大决策之前充分协商，尽可能就共同性问题取得一致意见。二者在不同层面和领域中发挥着不同的作用，相互补充、相得益彰，使民主效能大大提升。每年的人大、政协全国"两会"，就像超长"民主开放日"，让人们看到中国民主"双轮"的有效运转。

有事好商量，众人的事情由众人商量，找到全社会意愿和要求的最大公约数，是人民民主的真谛。"协商民主"就是充分体现这种精神的中国社会主义民主政治中独特的、独有的、独到的民主形式，它起源于80多年前中国共产党在陕北的实践。推进协商民主广泛多层制度化发展，是当下中国政治体制改革的重要内容。在中国，各项政策出台之所以较为顺利，是因为大量的矛盾或诉求在协商过程中已经得到了化解或吸纳。

1.4 价值逻辑：让人民自由

马克思指出，只有实现真正的民主，人类才能获得彻底的解放。马克思把他所要实现的共产主义理想社会界定为一种"自由人的联合体"，在那里，"每个人的自由发展是一切人的自由发展的条件"。

马克思以"每个人的自由发展"来界定"人的解放"，而人的"自由发展"则是最为重要的民主价值。按照马克思的理解，只有在人民当家作主的民主政治条件下，自由的价值才可能实现。

专栏：中国宪法中的民主自由人权

在现行中国宪法中，一共提到"民主"14次，"自由"13次，"人权"和"权利"共31次。

关于民主，宪法序言和总纲里提到新民主主义革命、社会主义民主、人民民主专政、民主党派、民主集中制、民主管理等。

关于自由，宪法第四条规定，各民族都有使用和发展自己的语言文字的自由，都有保持或者改革自己的风俗习惯的自由。

> 宪法第二章在公民的基本权利和义务中，提到公民有言论、出版、集会、结社、游行、示威的自由，宗教信仰自由、人身自由、通信自由、各种文化活动自由、婚姻自由等。
>
> 关于人权，宪法第三十三条规定，国家尊重和保障人权。宪法中共有九条涉及保护公民权利，包括财产、劳动与休息、受教育、女性、各民族，以及境内外国人、华侨等多方面权利。
>
> 资料来源：根据2018年3月修正的《中华人民共和国宪法》整理

从1840年鸦片战争到新中国成立前的痛苦经历，让中国人深深认识到，没有国家独立、民族解放，就没有真正的自由和人权。新中国的建立和社会主义制度的确立，从根本上消灭了阻碍人民享有自由的旧社会制度，人民的各种权利得到宪法保障。改革开放和发展社会主义市场经济，充分激发了全社会的创造活力，经济长期保持快速发展，人民生活日益富足。进入新时代，中国历史性地摆脱了绝对贫困，14亿多人口实现全面小康，人民对美好生活的向往不断变为现实，今天的中国人更加自信、自立、自强。

"自由意味着拥有一个可以使自己梦想成真的环境。"国际知名趋势研究者约翰·奈斯比特这样观察中国。[1]

---

[1]（美）约翰·奈斯比特、（德）多丽斯·奈斯比特：《中国大趋势：新社会的八大支柱》，吉林出版集团，2009年，第176页

全人类共同价值的追求与探索 — 民主自由人权的中国实践

对民主自由和人权的追求,也是中国发展和繁荣的动力。顺着"改革开放—脱贫攻坚—全面小康—共同富裕"的路线图,中国人摆脱贫困过上富足而尊严的生活,这是最大的政治,得益于全过程人民民主的落实。

中国的减贫成就

经过中共十八大以来**8年**持续奋斗到2020年底,中国现行标准下**9899万农村贫困人口**全部脱贫 → 832个贫困县全部摘帽 | 12.8万个贫困村全部出列

区域性整体贫困得到解决 ✓

改革开放以来,按照现行贫困标准计算,中国7.7亿农村贫困人口摆脱贫困

按照世界银行国际贫困标准
中国减贫人口占同期全球减贫人口**70%以上**

中国的减贫成就

脱贫攻坚战以来中国农村贫困人口变化情况

年份	贫困人口(万人)
2012年	9899
2013年	8249
2014年	7017
2015年	5575
2016年	4335
2017年	3046
2018年	1660
2019年	551
2020年	全部脱贫

资料来源:2021年4月发布的《人类减贫的中国实践》白皮书

第二章

全过程人民民主:落实人民主权的新形态

> 如果人民只有在投票时被唤醒、投票后就进入休眠期,只有竞选时聆听天花乱坠的口号、竞选后就毫无发言权,只有拉票时受宠、选举后就被冷落,这样的民主不是真正的民主。[1]
>
> ——习近平

---

[1] 习近平在中央人大工作会议上发表重要讲话,新华网,2021年10月14日

民主，意味着人民成为国家的主人，参与和管理国家和社会各项事务。在中国，人民有广泛参与国家治理的权利，体现在民主选举、民主协商、民主决策、民主管理、民主监督的各个环节。

这样一种"全过程人民民主"，追求的是过程民主和成果民主、程序民主和实质民主、直接民主和间接民主、人民民主和国家意志相统一。理解"全过程人民民主"，可以透过人、事、策、权四个维度。

2.1 "人"是怎么选的？

治理中国这样一个幅员辽阔、人口众多的国家，需要非常能干的国家领导人和各级官员。中国的选人机制，以德行、才干、绩效兼备为标准，层层选拔和民主选举相结合。加拿大政治学者贝淡宁认为，中国自古以来的贤能政治传统，是这一机制的文化底色。[1]

——选贤任能"金字塔"

有研究发现，在中国，干部一般都要从最基层做起，经过乡科、县处、厅局、省部等逐级晋升。从700多万干部中脱颖而出，成为正部级干部的几率只有1.4万分之一，平均所需时

---

[1] 该观点出自加拿大政治学者贝淡宁，参见《贤能政治》，中信出版社，2016年

间至少 23 年。[1]

不同于西方国家单纯靠选举产生的"空降兵"式的领导人，中国领导人的产生要经过一个一个政治台阶，层层选拔，出类拔萃，政绩卓著，经验丰富，才可能有效治理世界上人口最多的国家。[2]

中国共产党作为一个居于领导地位并得到中国宪法确认和保证的执政党，其内部的选贤任能竞争之激烈程度，超过了世界上其他所有的政治组织。[3]美国布鲁金斯学会约翰·桑顿中国中心主任李成发现，中国政治精英轮换的速度比率非常快，每五年一届的中央委员会中——近几届 60% 以上的委员都是新的。[4]这样的精英轮替在世界多国都属少见，有效保证了民主治理的竞争和优化。

——94% 直选率

很多人不知道，绝大多数中国基层民意代表是直接选举产生的。1954 年颁布的新中国首部宪法一步到位地实现了平等普

---

[1] 复兴之路工作室：《领导人是怎样炼成的》，2013 年 10 月 14 日
[2] 胡鞍钢：《政治局常委是如何产生的》，观察者网，2017 年 10 月 24 日
[3] 李世默：《中国式民主的强大生命力》，《人民日报（海外版）》，2013 年 4 月 1 日，第 1 版
[4] 袁静：《中国权力制衡机制与反腐败——专访美国布鲁金斯学会约翰·桑顿中国中心主任李成》，《人民论坛》，2014 年 12 期

遍的选举，逾 99% 的成年中国公民都有选举权和被选举权。而在同一时期，种族、性别等还是不少国家限制公民选举权的条件。

截至 2021 年 4 月，从国家到乡镇的中国五级人大代表，为数 262 万多名，其中占比 94% 的县乡人大代表，都是由选民一人一票直选产生。[1]

发挥各级人大代表作用是人民当家作主的重要体现，他们必须发挥好全过程人民民主的主体作用。这意味着，要不断丰富人大代表联系人民群众的内容和形式，以更密切地联系群众，反映好社情民意。

2.2 "事"是怎么议的？

全过程人民民主强调公民参与到公共政策决策全过程，即在决策前、决策中与决策后都能参与，努力做到人民知情权、参与权、表达权、监督权全覆盖，在集思广益中找到最优方案。

—— "立法直通车"

截至 2021 年 4 月，国家立法机关共有 230 件次法律草案向社会公开征求意见。全国人大常委会法工委近年设立了"基层立

---

[1] 《十三届全国人大四次会议举行新闻发布会 大会发言人张业遂答中外记者问》，新华网，2021 年 3 月 5 日

法联系点",使百姓意见抵达国家最高立法机关有了"直通车"。截至 2021 年 10 月,全国 22 个基层立法联系点共为 126 部法律草案、年度立法计划等提供 7800 余条意见建议,其中 2200 余条意见建议被不同程度吸收采纳,使立法更加精细化。[1]

其中的一条,来自上海的中学生李骏豪。2020 年 8 月,有关方面带着未成年人保护法修订草案,到华东政法大学附中征求意见,李骏豪同学提了一个意见:"每个未成年人家庭经济条件不一样,保证金处罚会使困难家庭'雪上加霜'。"他的建议得到全国人大常委会的采纳,最终通过的新修订的未成年人保护法,删去了草案中对未成年人监护人缴纳保证金的规定。

中国广泛征集民意程序

中共十八大以来
各民主党派中央、无党派人士向中共中央、国务院提出意见建议**730多件**
自2018年3月全国政协十三届一次会议至2021年4月
全国政协共收到提案**23048件**

截至2021年4月
国家立法机关共有**230件次**法律草案向社会公开征求意见

民法典草案公开征求意见期间
共收到**425762人次**提出的**1021834条**意见

资料来源:2021年6月发布的《中国共产党尊重和保障人权的伟大实践》白皮书

---

[1] 《架起百姓与最高立法机关的"连心桥"——全国人大常委会法工委基层立法联系点工作综述》,新华网,2021 年 11 月 2 日

——"民主恳谈会"

1999年发源于浙江温岭的"民主恳谈会",是一种通过充分协商来管理公共事务的"草根民主"。在当地,广大群众通过民主恳谈审议公共预算,企业职工通过民主恳谈进行工资集体协商,乡镇政府重大决策把民主恳谈作为必经程序。"遇到矛盾问题,就用民主恳谈",成了温岭人的习惯思维。

事实上,浙江德清的"乡贤参事会"、织里的"平安大姐工作室",上海长宁区"古北市民议事厅",江西赣州"屋场夜话",陕西西安长乐小区"'2+4'末梢治理"……中国各地创造出多种形式的基层协商民主,为实现善治发挥着重要作用。

2.3 "策"是怎么定的?

相当长的一个时期,中国的改革被称为"摸着石头过河",但令人好奇的是:为何中国常能摸对"石头"?这实际上反映了中国民主治理崇尚决策的科学性,例如中国国民经济和社会发展五年规划纲要等规划政策出台,就充分体现了民主决策的流程。同时,中央尊重基层首创精神,把基层创造的好经验上升为国家改革决策,以及,国家重大改革举措出台前交给部分地区"先行先试",取得经验再向全国推广。

——善用目标管理

中国执政者善于编制规划，运用目标管理和预期管理。新中国成立以来，中国已经编制实施14个五年规划（计划），"党提建议、政府编制规划、人大审议通过规划、全国人民执行人大审议通过的规划，这是中国共产党在国家治理当中创造的一个非常好的经验。"[1]

——基层经验

医改是世界难题。有14亿多人口的中国近年医改取得明显进展，一个重要原因是推广了地方首创经验——"三明模式"。福建省三明市推行医药、医保、医疗三医联动改革，有效破解了"看病难、看病贵"难题。基于三明的好做法，中国组建了国家医保局，推行集体采购实现药品和耗材大降价，百姓拍手称快。在中央提出"健康中国"新目标后，三明医改又积极推动医院从以"治病"为中心转向以"人民健康"为中心，新经验再次受到中央肯定并向全国推广。

——抗疫抉择

有些决策极为困难。2020年初新冠肺炎疫情突发，中国最

---

[1]《十九届五中全会，重要在哪？特殊在哪？——专访中央党校原副校长李君如》，中新网，2020年10月25日

高层作出武汉"封城"的决定，就是一例。为阻断疫情向全国蔓延，不得不对这座千万级人口城市的人员流动进行管控；中央同时决定，举全国之力支援武汉和它所在的湖北省，实施规模空前的生命大救援。不久，武汉、湖北和全国的疫情得到有效控制，取得了疫情防控阶段性胜利。

无论武汉封城，还是驰援武汉，决策的原则都是"人民至上""生命至上"。大疫之下，武汉人民以"隔一座城，护一国人"的担当，为全国战"疫"取得向好态势作出重大贡献；而全国人民奋力支援武汉，迅速遏制疫情，全力挽救生命，也让这座城市尽快重启，恢复了烟火气。"我为人人，人人为我"，中国人兼顾集体自由和个人自由的行动，让拍摄纪录片《好久不见，武汉》的日本导演竹内亮感叹："中国能成功实现既控制疫情又恢复经济，是全中国14亿多百姓一起努力的结果。"

2.4 "权"是怎么用的？

没有监督的权力必然导致腐败。权力是一把"双刃剑"，依法依规行使可以造福人民，违法违规行使必然祸害国家和人民。中国以党内监督、人大监督、民主监督、行政监督、司法监督、群众监督、舆论监督等一系列制度安排，依法设定权力、规范权力、制约权力、监督权力，把公权力关进制度的笼子。

——国家治理"哥德巴赫猜想"

中国共产党把实现自我监督比作国家治理的"哥德巴赫猜想",为求解这一难题进行制度创新,其中一项战略性安排就是"巡视"——中央向下级部门派出巡视组,赋予他们独立监督调查的权威,明确深化政治巡视,围绕党的政治建设、思想建设、组织建设、作风建设、纪律建设和夺取反腐败压倒性胜利等6个方面查找问题,将自上而下的组织监督和自下而上的群众监督有效结合起来,从而更加有利于发现问题,形成震慑效应。

——民主党派监督

民主监督在中国是多维的,一个特别的形式与中国新型政党制度有关。这一制度下,中国共产党与8个民主党派等展开合作,民主党派不是在野党、反对党,而是参与国家治理的参政党,被中国共产党视为"诤友"——能坦率提出批评建议的真朋友。

2016年以来,中国各民主党派中央对口八个贫困人口多、贫困发生率高的中西部省份,展开"脱贫攻坚民主监督",这是中国的民主党派首次对国家重大战略开展专项监督。他们向对口省份提出意见、批评、建议2400余条,向中共中央、国务院提交各类报告 80 余份，为打赢脱贫攻坚战发挥了重要作用。[1]

——国家权力监督新模式

"不得罪成百上千的腐败分子，就要得罪十三亿人民"[2]。基于这一认知，2012 年以来，中共掀起史上力度空前的反腐败风暴，打"老虎"（高官）无禁区，拍"苍蝇"（百姓身边的贪官）不手软，猎"狐狸"（逃到境外的贪腐分子）不止步，在制度上一体推进不敢腐、不能腐、不想腐，有效遏制了腐败蔓延势头，确保人民赋予的权力用来为人民谋幸福。

以 2018 年成立国家监察委员会和颁布监察法为标志，中国开启国家权力监督新模式，对全体党员和所有行使公权力的公职人员监督全覆盖，从根本上塑造规范、健康、常态化的反腐体系。

在 70 余年的探索实践中，中国形成了广泛、真实、管用的民主，走出了符合中国国情的民主发展道路。

---

[1] 国务院新闻办公室：《中国新型政党制度》白皮书，2021 年 6 月
[2] 习近平在第十八届中央纪律检查委员会第五次全体会议上的讲话，2015 年 1 月 13 日

> **专栏：中国的民主观**
>
> "人民当家作主"是中国的民主观。"全过程人民民主"是中国民主的基本特征，是全链条、全方位、全覆盖的民主，是最广泛、最真实、最管用的社会主义民主。这种民主坚持以人民为中心，超越"少数人民主""一次性民主""伪全民性民主"，确保广大人民群众真正享有民主权利，享受民主效果，确保民主理念深入人心。

第三章

管用的民主：判断制度成色的试金石

一个国家走的道路行不行，关键要看是否符合本国国情，是否顺应时代发展潮流，能否带来经济发展、社会进步、民生改善、社会稳定，能否得到人民支持和拥护，能否为人类进步事业作出贡献。[1]

——习近平

---

[1] 习近平在中华人民共和国恢复联合国合法席位 50 周年纪念会议上的讲话，2021 年 10 月 25 日

"不看广告，看疗效"，这句俗语反映的是一种务实态度。民主必须真实、管用，若不能转化为善政，为人民造福，即使有再华丽的外衣，再漂亮的包装，也是可疑的。

3.1 致善政的"治理型民主"

2020年6月，非政府组织"民主联盟"以及两家民意调查机构——"拉斯姆森全球"和德国达利亚研究院，联合发布民调显示：84%的中国人认为民主重要，同时高达73%的中国人认为自己的国家是民主国家，在53个被调查国家和地区中，排名第六；在"政府是否服务大多数"这个指标上，中国排名第二。[1]

这印证了许多观察者的结论：中国人认为民主应该是政府在作决策的时候，时刻想着最广大的人民利益，征求和听取人民意见，政府应该为人民服务。他们关心民主所要实现的目标，即良政善治，而不是多党制和普选。

---

[1] Democracy Perception Index 2020, Alliance of Democracies, Rasmussen Global, and Dalia Research, June 2021, https://www.allianceofdemocracies.org/initiatives/the-copenhagen-democracy-summit/dpi-2020/

——有效回应民意

中国人对民主的上述认知,与西方学者们的观点不谋而合:"不能回应民意的民主是无效的民主"(利普哈特),"好的民主一定是回应民意的民主"(萨托利),"理想的民主是选民对政治议程的最终控制"(罗伯特·达尔)。[1]

2020年,中国在"十四五"规划编制过程中,首次通过互联网向民众征求意见建议,101.8万条建言直通最高决策层。内蒙古达拉特旗大学生"村官"李电波惊讶地发现,自己上网提交的"互助养老"建议,被中央采纳。[2]

在"以人民为中心"的发展思想指导下,食品安不安全、暖气热不热、雾霾能不能少一点、河湖能不能清一点、能不能租得起或买得起住房……解决这些老百姓最关心的问题,都成为中国执政党的施政重点。

"中国共产党并不曾使用什么魔术,他们只不过知道人民所渴望的改变,而他们拥护这些改变。"早在1946年,美国记者白修德和贾安娜就注意到这一现象。[3]

中国共产党对人民的承诺不是以"竞选语言",而是以党

---

[1] 杨光斌:《让民主归位》,中国人民大学出版社,2015年,第95页

[2] 《第一观察:这位网友的建议写入了党中央文件》,新华网,2020年11月5日

[3] (美)白修德、贾安娜:《中国的惊雷》,新华出版社,1988年,序言第17-18页

的政策方针和决议的方式公布的，且承诺必须在实践中予以证明。"我说过，脱贫路上一个也不能少。"习近平 2021 年在广西的考察中说，"中国人说话、中国共产党说话、中国共产党的领导说话是算数的。"[1]

——治理导向

学者杨光斌认为，中国的民主是一种求善政的"治理民主"，它有三个要素：社会充分参与—国家自主性回应—负责任决策及其有效执行。"治理民主"不但重视政治过程的民主，更强调民主政治的结果即"良政"。[2]

中国的民主以治理为核心，而不是以选举为核心，因此在经济快速发展的同时保持了社会长期稳定，成为世界上最有安全感的国家之一。中国已确立国家治理体系和治理能力现代化的新目标，使各方面制度和国家治理更好体现人民意志、保障人民权益、激发人民创造力，民主发展的"治理导向"将进一步强化。

---

[1]《"加油、努力，再长征！"——习近平总书记考察广西纪实》，新华网，2021 年 4 月 29 日

[2] 杨光斌：《让民主归位》，中国人民大学出版社，2015 年，第 242 页

3.2 有活力的"效率型民主"

在中国这样一个发展中大国,如果没有人民的积极性主动性创造性,就没有社会活力;没有社会活力,就没有改革开放以来的巨大成就。同样,在中国这样一个情况极为复杂的国家,如果没有决策权威,也很难想象会有今天的局面。

——把"多种声音"合奏为"一首乐曲"

人们看到的是,"民主集中制"让中国充满活力又极具执行力。它既强调充分发扬民主,从而激发人民的积极性主动性创造性,又重视正确地集中——在民主基础上集思广益,形成科学决策并付诸实际行动。这是把"多种声音"合奏为"一首乐曲"的艺术,能够有效防止和克服议而不决、决而不行的分散主义,科学合理而有效率。[1]

民主集中制,既是中国共产党的组织原则,也是中国宪法中规定的各级国家机构所遵循的原则,还是一种决策的原则,体现于治国理政的方方面面,正越来越程序化、制度化。

中国国务院2019年施行的《重大行政决策程序暂行条例》,确认合法性审查和集体讨论决定是所有重大行政决策的必经程序,决策机关行政首长要在集体讨论基础上作出决定。

---

[1] 习近平:《之江新语》,浙江人民出版社,2007年,第22页

3.3 汇众智的"动力型民主"

中国在实践中认识到,中国特色社会主义是亿万人民自己的事业,所以必须发挥人民主人翁精神,更好保证人民当家作主。这意味着,民主也是动力,为了人民而发展,发展才有意义,依靠人民而发展,发展才有动力。

——调动人民积极性是最大民主

坚持人民主体地位,充分调动人民积极性,被中国共产党视为立于不败之地的强大根基。邓小平有句名言:调动积极性是最大的民主。可以说,没有民主,就没有中国奇迹。通过政治、经济等全方位改革扩大民主,激发亿万人民的积极性主动性创造性,发展生产力,让人民真正参与到改革和社会建设当中,是中国改革开放后现代化建设提速的重要原因。

发端于安徽省凤阳县小岗村的家庭联产承包责任制就是一个典型案例。1978年一个冬夜,低矮破旧的茅草屋里,十八位村民摁下红手印签订契约,把村集体田地分到各家单干。这一创举逐渐席卷全国,几亿农民的积极性被充分调动起来,打开了中国农村改革的新局面。中国的改革开放是从发扬民主开始的——关于真理标准的全国大讨论,使"实践是检验真理的唯一标准"得以确立,社会空前活跃起来,生产力不断解放和发展,制度体制的改革与创新成为常态。

全人类共同价值的追求与探索 · 一 民主自由人权的中国实践

交通便利让出行更自由

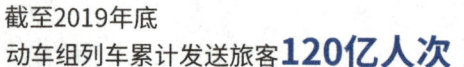

截至2019年底
动车组列车累计发送旅客 **120亿人次**

 占铁路旅客发送量的比重
由2007年的 **4.5%** 增长到 **65.4%**

资料来源：2020年12月发布的《中国交通的可持续发展》白皮书

基础设施从"连线成片"到"基本成网"

 截至2019年底
全国铁路营业里程达到 **13.9万公里**
其中高速铁路营业里程超过 **3.5万公里**

全国公路里程达到 **501.3万公里**
其中高速公路里程 **15万公里**

资料来源：2020年12月发布的《中国交通的可持续发展》白皮书

——发展与自由互动

中国坚持以发展为人"赋能"，持续扩大"对人的投资"，为人民自由发展提供更多可能性。与之相伴的是，自由拓展带来生产力的进一步解放，以及人力资本、社会资本的增加，为国家发展注入推动力，实现了发展与自由的相互促进与转化。

中国的实践表明，发展是扩展人们享有的真实自由的过程。"远在实行经济改革之前，中国就一直是在当代世界——特别是通过教育普及、医疗保健和土地改革上的重大进步——促进社会变革的先行者。中国在改革后取得了令人瞩目的经济进步，社会进步与经济发展之间的互补性在中国经验中得到了很好说明。"诺贝尔经济学奖得主阿马蒂亚·森这样认为。[1]

——梦想照亮现实

今天，中国的全面发展进步，为每个人追逐梦想提供了广阔空间。每个人为了美好梦想而奋斗，汇聚起实现中国梦的磅礴力量。中国梦，是个人理想与中华民族伟大复兴梦想的有机融合，是人的全面发展与国家整体进步的高度统一。中国梦，为14亿多中国人追求民主自由和发展人权事业描绘出崭新愿景，也将激发人民贡献自己的智慧与力量。

过去一百年，中国共产党向人民交出了一份优异答卷。现在，又团结带领人民踏上了实现第二个百年奋斗目标新的赶考之路。民主是一道必答题，因为，"没有民主就没有社会主义，就没有社会主义的现代化，就没有中华民族伟大复兴。"[2]

---

[1]（印）阿马蒂亚·森：《以自由看待发展》，中国人民大学出版社，2013年，中文版序言
[2] 习近平在庆祝全国人民代表大会成立六十周年大会上的讲话，2014年9月5日

3.4 可检验的"系统性民主"

评价一种政治制度是否民主、先进,并非易事,其难点在于缺少客观全面的标准。中国提出了衡量民主的八条标准,引起人们的关注。

——"八个能否"民主标准[1]

> **专栏:民主的"八个能否"标准**
>
> ◎国家领导层能否依法有序更替
> ◎全体人民能否依法管理国家事务和社会事务、管理经济和文化事业
> ◎人民群众能否畅通表达利益要求
> ◎社会各方面能否有效参与国家政治生活
> ◎国家决策能否实现科学化、民主化
> ◎各方面人才能否通过公平竞争进入国家领导和管理体系
> ◎执政党能否依照宪法法律规定实现对国家事务的领导
> ◎权力运用能否得到有效制约和监督

---

[1] "八个能否"民主标准出自"习近平在庆祝全国人民代表大会成立六十周年大会上的讲话",2014年9月5日

政治学者们认为，"八个能否"标准总结了中外民主政治发展的经验教训，符合现代政治文明原则，反映了全过程人民民主的系统性，在世界范围看，这是一种扎根深厚现实基础的理论探索：[1]

一种综合民主观——从多个维度、多个层面观察政治制度，判断是否属于民主、民主实现程度的标准尺度不应是单一的、片面的，而应是综合的、整体的评价。

一种发展民主观——民主制度是一个持续不断的发展和演进过程，不断从低级走向高级、从传统走向现代，民主建设是进行时，没有最好、只有更好。

一种实效民主观——坚持形式民主与实质民主、程序民主与实体民主、间接民主与直接民主相结合，从诸多方面实际效果和结果对政治制度进行客观评价。[2]

连续十余年，哈佛大学肯尼迪政府学院阿什民主治理与创新中心的研究显示，民众对中国共产党的信任度超过90%。[3]

另据加拿大约克大学的一项调查，中国民众对中央政府的

---

[1] 复旦大学政党建设与国家发展研究中心主任郑长忠接受新华社记者采访，2021年9月

[2] 沈春耀：《民主政治展现新境界 依法治国开启新征程》，《中国人大》，2016年第7期

[3] Edward Cunningham, Tony Saich & Jesse Turiel, Understanding CCP Resilience: Surveying Chinese Public Opinion Through Time, Harvard Kennedy School Ash Center, July 2020

满意度高达 98%，对地方政府的满意度也超过 90%。[1]

  一些敏锐的国际观察者得出结论，在西方很少有人意识到：中国共产党已经为中国提供了历史上的最佳治理。新加坡前外长杨荣文说，民主的实质，意味着人民的政府，"根据这一定义，中国是一个民主国家"。[2]

---

[1] 《美媒：民调显示中国民众对政府信任度高达 98%》，参考消息网，2021 年 5 月 8 日

[2] 《新加坡前外交部长杨荣文接受〈环球时报〉专访：中国有自己实现民主理念的途径》，环球网，2021 年 6 月 8 日

第四章

实践智慧：追求全人类共同价值的启示

> 我们要秉持人类命运共同体理念，坚守和平、发展、公平、正义、民主、自由的全人类共同价值，摆脱意识形态偏见，最大程度增强合作机制、理念、政策的开放性和包容性，共同维护世界和平稳定。[1]
>
> ——习近平

---

[1] 习近平在世界经济论坛"达沃斯议程"对话会上的特别致辞，2021年1月25日

全人类共同价值的追求与探索 —— 民主自由人权的中国实践

全人类共同价值是人类在长期社会化过程中彼此联系、相互交往的必然结果，也是人类历史从民族走向世界的必然产物。它是人类文明的共同财富，是破解当今时代难题的钥匙，也是建设更加美好世界的最大公约数。

中国共产党带领人民在一穷二白的基础上进行的超大规模民主实践，以及对自由、人权的不懈追求，不仅是为中国人民谋幸福、为中华民族谋复兴，也着眼于为人类谋进步、为世界谋大同。中国通过推动自身发展给世界创造了更多机遇，也通过深化自身实践探索着人类社会发展规律。

中国实践表明，民主、自由、人权相互联系、相互依赖、相互促进。良好的民主是自由和人权的保障，拥有自由和人权的人民，是维护民主和推动进步的能动力量。三者当中，民主可以落实为制度载体，抓住民主建设的"牛鼻子"，人民的自由和权利就有了制度保障。

如果说追求全人类共同价值是"做正确的事"，那么，"把正确的事做正确"，则是巨大的实践挑战。中国走出的民主自由人权之路，提供了有益的知识启示。

4.1 "致治"之道：三个"关键应用"

中国追求民主自由人权的实践在两大背景中展开，一方面是本国追求现代化的发展进程，另一方面是全球化的世界大潮。

哈佛大学教授丹尼·罗德里克曾提出著名的全球化三元悖论："经济全球化，国家自主权和民主无法同时实现。"[1] 而中国的现实则为这样的论断提供了反证。过去数十年来，中国加入全球化，始终坚持独立自主的发展道路，同时创造性地发展了中国特色社会主义民主。这背后反映出强大的国家治理能力。包括"历史终结论"提出者弗朗西斯·福山在内，越来越多政治学家认识到，在21世纪的全球治理中，国家治理能力至关重要。

民主、自由和人权在中国的实践，形成了一系列行之有效的治理思想与方法。先进政党、人民至上、聚焦发展或可喻为中国"致治"之道的三大"关键应用"。

App 1：先进政党

读懂今天的中国，必须读懂中国共产党。"坚持党的集中统一领导，坚持党的科学理论，保持政治稳定，确保国家始终沿着社会主义方向前进"[2]，在中国国家制度和国家治理体系的显著优势中，居于首位。

---

[1]（英）爱德华·卢斯：《西方自由主义的衰落》，山西人民出版社，2019年，第70页

[2]《中共中央关于坚持和完善中国特色社会主义制度 推进国家治理体系和治理能力现代化若干重大问题的决定》，2019年10月31日中国共产党第十九届中央委员会第四次全体会议通过

全人类共同价值的追求与探索 — 民主自由人权的中国实践

中国共产党是一个特别意义上的政党,它代表的是最广大人民根本利益,不代表任何利益集团、任何权势团体、任何特权阶层的利益,其治国理政着眼国家长治久安,而非为了短期选举竞斗。作为先进政党的显著特征,中国共产党始终站在人民利益角度,顺应人类和时代进步的大潮流,总揽全局、协调各方,团结组织各派政治力量、各种政治资源,为全体人民谋幸福、为中华民族谋复兴,有着自己的行动逻辑。

与外界误解的所谓"一党独裁"不同,中国的新型政党制度可以理解为"1+8+N"的民主实践。中国除了中国共产党外还有 8 个民主党派,这些参政的政党人数虽然不多,但都是有影响力的人士,尤其以知识分子居多。他们的参政议政,为执政党决策提供了不可或缺的知识贡献。在"1"和"8"之外,还有无党派人士,以及广大人民群众。他们可以通过各种途径参与国家的民主议程。

一党领导,确保了执政权威、民主决策的效率和政策连续性;多党协商,使中国的决策能广纳贤能,汇集众智;全民献力,使执政者能团结最大多数的人民力量。民主与集中的有机聚合,有效降低了政治资源内耗。党内监督和不断发展的社会监督,从内外双向保证了民主的问责。

中国共产党为中国人民享有民主、自由、人权进行了艰苦卓绝的斗争,创造了一个又一个给人民带来福祉的奇迹。中国共产党具有高度觉悟性、纪律性和自我牺牲精神,能够真正代表和团结人民群众，具有足够的权威。中国共产党的领导，对中国这样一个超大规模国家的治理至关重要。正如中国改革开放总设计师邓小平所言，"没有这样一个党的统一领导，是不可能设想的，那就只会四分五裂，一事无成"。[1]

App 2：人民至上

"民无信不立"。2000多年前的中国圣贤孔子，就指出了好政府（执政者）的关键标准。民心，就是人民对执政者的信任。把"以人民为中心"作为制定政策的出发点，政治的成效才有可能得到人民的信任。"民心是最大的政治"，成为中国执政党的信条。

今天，大约每10个成年中国人当中，就有1个中共党员。他们遍布在各个家庭、身边邻里。党的宗旨——全心全意为人民服务，党的初心使命——为人民谋幸福、为民族谋复兴，党的价值追求——以人民为中心、人民至上，中国共产党与人民的血肉联系，彰显了权力的来源和归宿。

"以人民为中心"使中国"政道"和"治道"获得稳固的价值坐标。在现代中国社会的治理中，"服务"成为关键词，"人民满意度"成为政绩新标尺，政府与社会正在形成新契约。

---

[1]《邓小平文选》第二卷，人民出版社，1994年，第341-342页

全人类共同价值的追求与探索 — 民主自由人权的中国实践

中国人口人均寿命增长情况

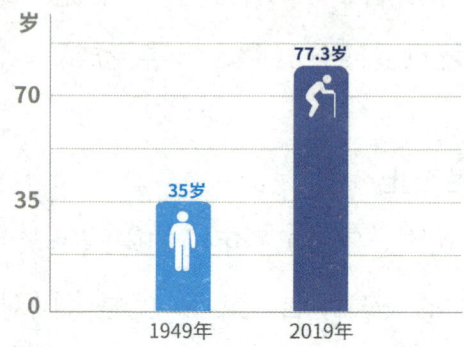

2019年，中国居民平均预期寿命从1949年的 **35岁** 提高到 **77.3岁**

中国住房面积、医疗条件的改善

 中国城镇居民和农村居民人均住房建筑面积在改革开放之初分别为 **6.7平方米** 和 **8.1平方米**，2019年分别增长到 **39.8平方米** 和 **48.9平方米**

 2020年，**基本医疗保险**覆盖达 **13.6亿人**

 2018年，全国共有卫生机构 **99.7万个**，比1949年增长 **271.78倍**

 把贫困人口全部纳入 **基本医疗保险、大病保险、医疗救助** 三重制度保障范围，贫困人口基本医疗保险参保率稳定在 **99.9%以上**

中国人入学率、文盲率、高等教育率情况

新中国成立之初
教育水平低，人口文化素质差
小学净入学率和初中毛入学率仅分别为 **20%和3%**
高校在校生仅有 **11.7万人**，全国 **80%** 的人口是文盲

全国高中阶段教育毛入学率从2000年的 **42.8%** 提高到2020年的 **91.2%**

高等教育毛入学率从2000年的 **12.5%** 提高到2020年的 **54.4%**
高等教育在学总规模超过 **4000万人**
建成世界上 **最大规模** 的高等教育体系

资料来源：2021年6月发布的《中国共产党尊重和保障人权的伟大实践》白皮书、
2019年9月发布的《为人民谋幸福：新中国人权事业发展70年》白皮书、
2021年8月发布的《全面建成小康社会：中国人权事业发展的光辉篇章》白皮书

—— "治商"

人民拥护不拥护、赞成不赞成、高兴不高兴、答应不答应，是衡量一切工作得失的根本标准。把这个标准放诸国家治理效能中，中国社会呈现出高"治商"特点，其标准，简而言之，体现为人民的安全感、获得感和幸福感。与"三感"相对应，是国家治理的安民、富民、乐民能力。中国的民主自由人权实践的不断进步，就以无可辩驳的事实表明，人民至上的治理价值观在中国绝非政治口号。

App 3：聚焦发展

"中国的世界观聚焦于发展"。美国兰德公司2020年3月的一份报告敏锐观察，这种世界观，很可能使中国在21世纪的国家竞争中形成独特的优势。

70多年来，党和国家聚焦发展，使中国人获得了越来越多的自由和民主权利。更多的自由和民主权利，进一步促进了整个国家的发展。而发展的成效继续完善民主治理，使人民的权利得到更好保障。发展与自由的辩证法，民主与人权的互动性，在中国实践中得到生动体现。这样的中国变量，通过全球化，传导到世界，增益了全球福祉。

"中国坚定维护多边主义，维护公平正义，维护《联合国宪章》的宗旨和原则，发挥了重要的稳定作用，给世界以确定性、信心和希望。"联合国秘书长古特雷斯认为，历史将证明，中国的发展不仅是不可阻挡的历史潮流，也是对人类文明进步的重大贡献。

中国城乡收入比变化

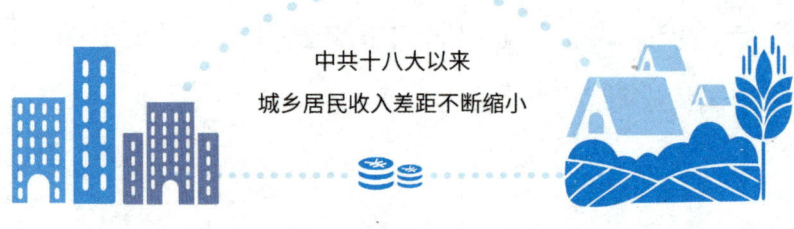

城乡居民人均可支配收入之比2018年已下降至 **2.69**

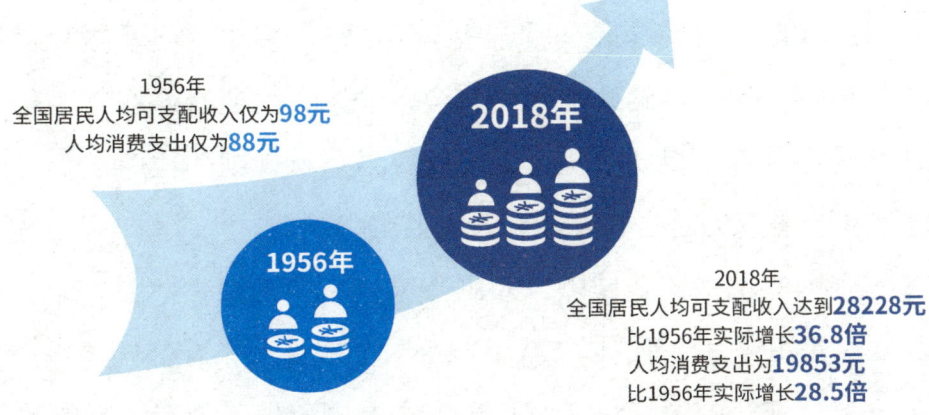

资料来源：2019年9月发布的《为人民谋幸福：新中国人权事业发展70年》白皮书

4.2 实现全人类共同价值："四项原则"

仰望全人类共同价值和理想，又脚踏实地上下求索，新中国70多年来取得的发展与稳定奇迹表明，中国是民主自由人权"忠实的实践者"和"实践的创新者"，为实现全人类共同价值提供了有益启示。

——实践原则

"理论是灰色的，而生活之树常青"。丰富生动的实践，是民主自由和人权创新的理论之源。理论、制度设计是否有效，必须通过实践来检验和完善。一个国家民主不民主，关键在于

全人类共同价值的追求与探索 —— 民主自由人权的中国实践

是不是真正做到了人民当家作主，要看人民有没有投票权，更要看人民有没有广泛参与权；要看人民在选举过程中得到了什么口头许诺，更要看选举后这些承诺实现了多少；要看制度和法律规定了什么样的政治程序和政治规则，更要看这些制度和法律是不是真正得到了执行；要看权力运行规则和程序是否民主，更要看权力是否真正受到人民监督和制约。[1]

中国的民主实践，以"人民当家作主"为初心，以"全过程人民民主"为特征，以"八个能否"为标准，以"走自己的路"为方法，富有中国特色又践行全人类共同价值，创造了新的政治文明形态。

——自主原则

民主是各国人民的权利，而不是少数人、少数国家的专利。一个国家是不是民主、人民有没有自由、人权是否得到了保障，应该由这个国家的人民来评判，而不应该由外部少数人指手画脚来评判。国际社会哪个国家是不是民主的、自由的，人民是否享受充分人权，也应该由国际社会共同来评判，而不应该由自以为是的少数国家来评判。各国人民有权选择自己的发展道路和制度模式，这本身就是人民幸福的应有之义，也符合民主的精神。把自己的民主自由人权观强加于人，本

---

[1] 习近平在中央人大工作会议上发表重要讲话，新华网，2021年10月14日

身就违反了民主自由人权的真精神。当今国际形势的发展证明了中国的观点：外部军事干涉和所谓的"民主改造"贻害无穷。

各国发展民主，必须走出教条主义和话语霸权的迷雾，独立自主地探索自己的路。成功的民主建构都各具特色，民主生成方式、组织方式以及运行方式的多样性，正是现代政治文明生命力和创造力的根本所在。必须使民主深深扎根于中国社会土壤，不能指望从外国搬来一座政治制度上的"飞来峰"就万事大吉。照抄照搬他国政治制度的结果，会"画虎不成反类犬"，没实现民主，倒实现了"民苦"，甚至葬送国家的前途命运。

——时序原则

实现民主自由和发展人权事业，是有前提，有顺序，也是需要基础的，不同国家要根据各自的国情循序渐进，既不能丧失机遇，也不能超越发展阶段，否则"欲速则不达"。要统筹考虑多种因素，兼顾改革力度、发展速度与社会可承受度，制订行动的路线图和时间表。许多输入外国民主模式导致的"失败国家"，一个重要原因，就在于没有根据自身实际统筹好发展与时序的关系，因而造成社会失序、政局动荡等一系列问题，经济社会发展一再遭遇挫折。

全人类共同价值的追求与探索 —— 民主自由人权的中国实践

中国人的就业、养老条件

截至2020年底,全国就业人数为 **75064万人**
中国建成世界上**规模最大**的社会保障体系

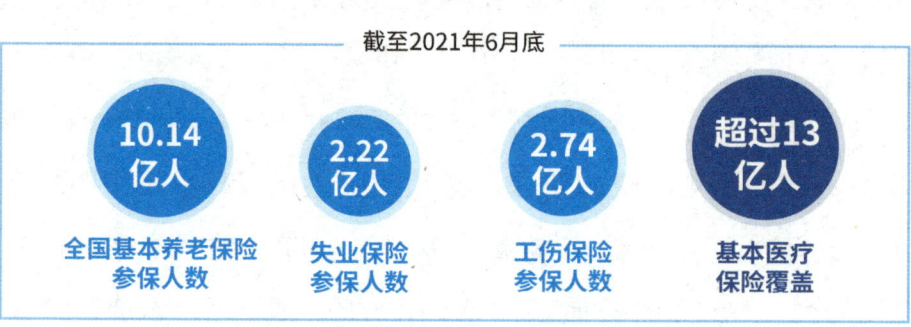

资料来源:2021年8月发布的《中国共产党的历史使命与行动价值》

专栏:中国的新时代人权观

"人民幸福生活是最大的人权"是中国的新时代人权观。2021年开始实施的第四期中国"国家人权行动计划",提出了新议程:坚持以人民为中心的发展思想,将促进人的全面发展、全体人民共同富裕作为人权事业发展的出发点和落脚点,发展全过程人民民主,维护社会公平正义,着力解决人民群众急难愁盼问题,使全体人民的各项人权得到更高水平的保障,不断增强人民对于人权保障的获得感、幸福感、安全感。

中国的人权发展,基于生存权发展权是首要的基本人权,不断向内容更丰富、水平更高的"人民幸福生活是最大的人权"这一塔尖攀登。

——过程原则

追求民主自由和尊重保障人权是一个止于至善的发展过程，没有完成时，只有进行时，没有最好，只有更好。西方的民主实践开启了人类现代民主进程，但这并不意味着人类的民主发展会终结于西方模式。民主自由和人权的实现，必须随着实践发展而发展，必须本土化才能落地生根、深入人心。不同国家人民的探索，会不断充实和改善人类民主自由和人权实践，使全人类共同价值在内涵日益丰富中生动起来，而不会因逐渐"空心化"而枯萎下去。

> **专栏：中国的自由观**
>
> 中国在实践中不断解放和发展生产力，形成了以"人的全面发展"为内涵的中国自由观。中国自由观赋予人民极大物质和精神自由，推动人的自由全面发展，并在实践路径上着力统筹公平与效率、有序与活力、权力与权利等关系，实现共同理想与个人追求、集体主义与个人发展、统一意志与个人自由的辩证统一。

4.3 "时代之问"：中国方案

"世界怎么了，我们怎么办？"2017年1月18日，中国国家主席习近平在联合国日内瓦总部发出"时代之问"。

全人类共同价值的追求与探索 —— 民主自由人权的中国实践

大疫之下，历史大变革的关口，文明如何发展，人类如何共处？2021年10月25日，中华人民共和国恢复联合国合法席位50周年，习近平主席给出新的思考：我们应该大力弘扬和平、发展、公平、正义、民主、自由的全人类共同价值，共同为建设一个更加美好的世界提供正确理念指引。和平与发展是我们的共同事业，公平正义是我们的共同理想，民主自由是我们的共同追求。

——回到"常识"

当今世界，民主变质、自由变形、人权变味，多国的治理现状令人不安。"民主的贫困"已是不争事实，既表现为极化政治、贫富分化、治理失灵、国际霸凌等种种现实危机，也表现为"自由民主理论"难以解释现实，更不要说解决问题了。这正如学者所描述的"范式危机"的情境，人类需要新的框架和知识来突破困境，找到在一个全球化时代实现全人类共同价值的路。

民主不等于善治，甚至会导致动荡，这现实的危机发人深思。如果要"加强"和"更新"民主，必须先回到"常识"——什么是民主？正如中国的实践所表明的，民主的真正含义乃是人民当家作主，追求平等与公正，实现国家良治和人民福祉，在国际关系中"一国的事情由本国人民做主，国际上的事情由大家商量着办"。[1]

14亿多人为实现民主自由人权艰辛探索获得的认知，不应被忽视。民主自由人权发展的中国之"道"，为解决人类的民主贫困、自由困境、人权挑战治理赤字提振了信心，增加了认知，注入了动力，贡献了方法。

——多样性不仅合理而且美好

和平、发展、公平、正义、民主、自由是全人类共同价值，但其实现路径是个性化的，应该尊重不同国家人民对价值实现路径的探索，把全人类共同价值具体地、现实地体现到实现本国人民利益的实践中去。那种唯我独尊，执意用某种模式改造甚至取代其他文明的做法，认识上是愚蠢的，做法上是专制的，结果更是灾难性的，教训已经够多。

人类文明多样性赋予这个世界姹紫嫣红的色彩，多样带来交流，交流孕育融合，融合产生进步。多样性不仅合乎常理，而且美好，"各美其美，美美与共"，各国应该在"和而不同"的民主政治和人权的实践中，交流互鉴，共同驱动人类文明的进步。以全人类共同价值为指引的意义，正如2022年北京冬奥会、冬残奥会主题口号传递的期待："一起向未来"。

---

[1] 习近平出席上海合作组织和集体安全条约组织成员国领导人阿富汗问题联合峰会并发表重要讲话，新华网，2021年9月17日

——人类命运共同体

有人曾以为，国家就是最大的政治单位，世界只是空洞的地理空间，而今天的真相是：人类是一个整体，居住的星球是一个"地球村"，任何国家都无法独善其身。世界多极化、国际关系民主化是大势所趋，人类只有抓住历史机遇，作出正确选择，才能开创更加光明的未来。从"大道之行，天下为公"到"人类命运共同体"，中国的"天下一家"观，为徘徊于十字路口的世界指明了正确的方向。

民主自由是全人类共同价值的核心内容，人权是各国人民为之不懈奋斗的理想。在捍卫民主自由人权的社会主义实践中，中国共产党一切政治行动都以人民整体利益为基本取向，让民主回归人民的逻辑，让自由成全人的全面发展，让幸福成为人权的最高标准，开辟了国家现代化新道路，开创了人类文明新形态，为"时代之问"提交了一份具有世界意义的中国方案。

结　语

　　和平、发展、公平、正义、民主、自由这些全人类共同价值是构建人类命运共同体的价值基础。"条条大路通罗马",实现这些人类共通的理想追求,需要各国根据各自国情不断探索最适合本国人民根本利益的最佳路径。

　　在中西方文明的碰撞交融中,中国找到了"中国特色社会主义"这条实践证明卓有成效的中国式现代化道路。正如中国领导人习近平所指出的,"当代中国的伟大社会变革,不是简单延续我国历史文化的母版,不是简单套用马克思主义经典作家设想的模板,不是其他国家社会主义实践的再版,也不是国外现代化发展的翻版"。

　　中国促进民主、维护自由、保障人权不断取得进步,但前路仍然充满挑战,14亿多人口走向物质和精神层面的共同富裕,仍需要不断推进国家治理体系和治理能力的现代化,不断加强与各国的交流互鉴,携手共同推进人类进步事业。

　　探索无止境,追求无终点……

编写说明与致谢

《全人类共同价值的追求与探索：民主自由人权的中国实践》智库报告由新华通讯社社长、新华社国家高端智库学术委员会主任何平任组长，总编辑傅华任副组长，副社长张宿堂任课题负责人，课题组成员包括孙承斌、刘刚、班玮、储国强、顾钱江、刘丽娜、崔峰、叶书宏、郝薇薇、刘阳、宣力祺、宗巍、李怀岩、梁建强、陈尚营、周蕊、闫睿、刘明霞等。

在报告写作过程中，国务院新闻办公室原主任赵启正；中共中央党校原副校长李君如；中央党史研究室原副主任章百家；中国人权研究会秘书长鲁广锦；中国人民大学国际关系学院院长杨光斌、法学院教授朱力宇、马克思主义学院副教授张飞岸、国家发展与战略研究院副教授刁大明；中国社科院政治学研究所所长张树华、当代中国政治研究室主任樊鹏；中国国际问题研究院院长徐步；外交学院副院长高飞；全球化智库（CCG）理事长王辉耀；北京大学国际关系学院院长唐士其、国学研究院教授徐建委；清华大学国学研究院院长陈来、国情研究院副院长鄢一龙；复旦大学国际关系与公共事务学院教授唐世平、陈周旺、韩福国、副教授郑长忠，法学院教授马忠法、副教授陆志安；华东师范大学哲学系教授陈赟、政治与国际关系学院副院长刘军、副研究员阎德学；华中科技大学国家治理研究院院长欧阳康、人权法律研究院院长汪习根、马克思主义学院院长岳奎、新闻与信息传播学院院长张明新；山东大学政治学与公共管理学院院长贝淡宁、国家治理研究院副院长孔新峰；内蒙古师范大学党委书记阿拉坦仓；吉林大学人权研究中心执行主任何志鹏；西南政法大学人权研究院副院长孟庆涛；社科院马克思主义研究院副研究员宋丽丹、孟庆友等专家学者给予了大力协助和指导，在此一并表示感谢。

在报告撰写过程中，由于所掌握的材料和作者水平有限，错漏之处在所难免，敬请广大读者批评指正。

新华社大型纪录片《共同的追求：民主自由人权的身边故事》之《恳谈会》

新华社大型纪录片《共同的追求：民主自由人权的身边故事》之《慢火车》

新华社大型纪录片《共同的追求：民主自由人权的身边故事》之《听电影》

新华社大型纪录片《共同的追求:民主自由人权的身边故事》之《望夕阳》

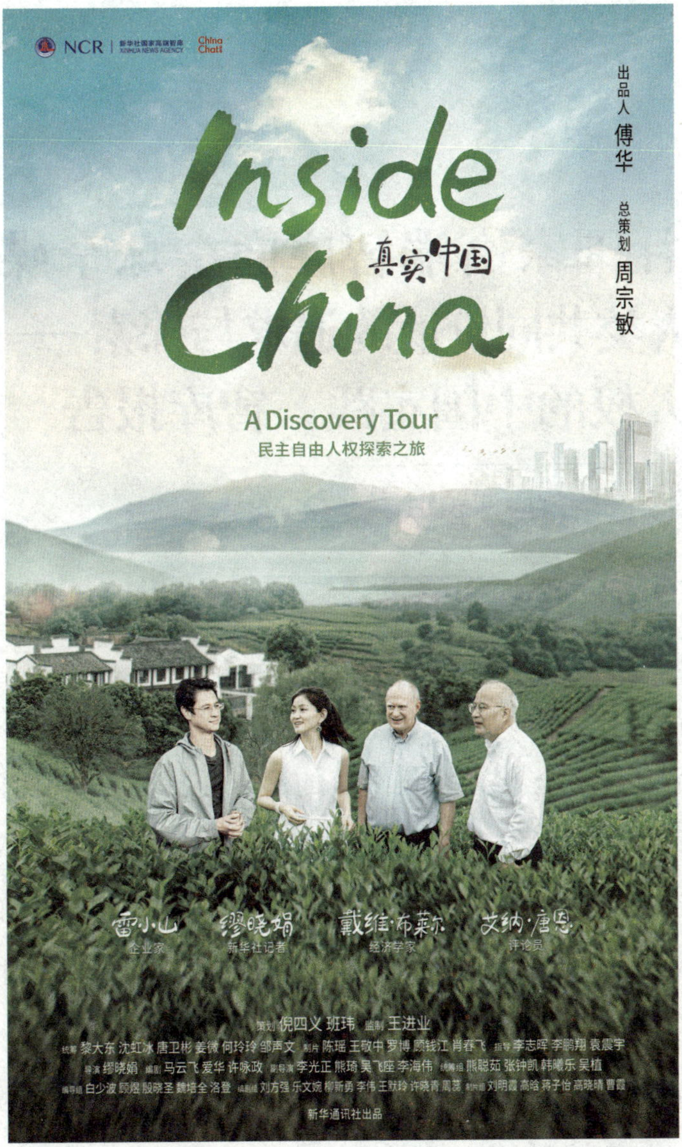

欢迎扫码观看
新华社重磅纪录片《真实中国：
民主自由人权探索之旅》

附 录

新华社国家高端智库向全球全媒发布《全人类共同价值的追求与探索——民主自由人权的中国实践》智库报告

新华社国家高端智库课题组

新华社国家高端智库 2021 年 12 月 7 日向全球全媒发布中英文智库报告《全人类共同价值的追求与探索——民主自由人权的中国实践》及纪录片，深度解读中国共产党高举人民民主旗帜、实现人民当家作主，中国人民成为国家、社会和自己命运的主人的伟大成就，深刻阐释中国人民始终不渝追求全人类共同价值的历史逻辑、实践逻辑和理论逻辑。

智库报告和纪录片当日在北京和瑞士日内瓦正式发布。来自亚洲、非洲、欧洲和南美洲等 40 多个国家和地区的近百名智库机构的专家、学者线上或线下参会。报告中的主要观点和典型案例等，将以中、英、西、俄、阿、葡、蒙古文等多语种在多国媒体上传播。

附 录

  全文 1.9 万字的报告以习近平总书记关于全人类共同价值的重要论述为主线,以中国追求全人类共同价值的长期实践为基础,从学理角度阐释中国实现人民当家作主的制度优势、文化背景、内在规律及其世界意义,围绕"人民当家作主:追求民主价值的大逻辑""全过程人民民主:落实人民主权的新形态""管用的民主:判断制度成色的试金石"和"实践智慧:追求全人类共同价值的启示"4 个部分展开。

全人类共同价值的追求与探索 —— 民主自由人权的中国实践

中国的民主是人民民主，人民当家作主是中国民主的本质和核心。为实现人民当家作主，中国始终坚持以人民为中心，超越"少数人民主""一次性民主""伪全民性民主"，确保最广大人民群众真正享有民主权利，让人民真正成为国家、社会和自己命运的主人。报告通过大量事例证明，中国追求人民当家作主的"实质民主"，是全链条、全方位、全覆盖的"全过程人民民主"，致善政的"治理型民主"，有活力的"效率型民主"，汇众智的"动力型民主"，可检验的"系统性民主"，是最广泛、最真实、最管用的社会主义民主。

报告认为，中国追求全人类共同价值的长期实践得出的结论是：从人民的视角出发，民主治理的好坏只有一个标准——老百姓能够享受和平发展的红利，过上安宁祥和的幸福生活。良好的民主治理，能使自由和人权得到保障和发展，能实现过程民主和成果民主、程序民主和实质民主、直接民主和间接民主、人民民主和国家意志有机统一。

民主不是装饰品，不是用来做摆设的。报告指出，中国是民主、自由、人权理念"忠实的实践者"和"实践的创新者"。中国在人民当家作主的实践中，取得了显著的治理成效，具有高"治商"。解码中国民主的"致治"之道，或可将先进政党、人民至上、聚焦发展概括为"三大关键应用"。

报告认为，在捍卫民主、自由、人权的社会主义实践中，中国共产党将一切政治行为都以人民整体利益为基本取向，让民主回归人民的逻辑、让自由成全人的全面发展、让幸福成为人权的最高标准，开辟了国家现代化新道路，开创了人类文明新形态，为"时代之问"提交了一份具有世界意义的"中国方案"。

报告指出，中国的探索追求表明，民主的有效性必须通过能否解决绝大多数人实际问题的实践来检验和完善的"实践原则"，民主、自由、人权的路径选择必须基于本国国情的"自主原则"，促进民主、维护自由、保障人权需要循序渐进的"时序原则"，民主、自由、人权的追求没有最好只有更好的"过程原则"，可为实现全人类共同价值提供有益借鉴。

新华社国家高端智库专题课题组深入中国东、中、西部近30个省、区、市开展深入调研，广泛采访国内外专家学者和各方面人士，并组织召开多次专题研讨会，经过总结提炼，最终形成这一报告。权威人士研读后认为，智库报告调研扎实、说理透

全人类共同价值的追求与探索 — 民主自由人权的中国实践

彻,对全人类共同价值作出了新的学理化阐释和学术化表达。

中英文文字报告发布的同时,由新华社国家高端智库制作的中英文双语纪录片《共同的追求——民主自由人权的身边故事》同步上线,六名普通的中国人以亲身经历讲述了发生在中国大地上的民主、自由、人权的生动故事。与智库报告同名图书及相关可视化产品也即将面向海内外出版发行。

新华社国家高端智库是中国国家高端智库方阵中唯一媒体型智库,近年来形成了众多有影响的智库研究成果,此前已推出《中国减贫学》《人民标尺》等专题智库报告,在海内外产生广泛影响。

驻日内瓦外交官和专家对中国民主理论和实践予以高度评价

新华社记者

新华社国家高端智库 2021 年 12 月 7 日在中国北京和瑞士日内瓦同步发布《全人类共同价值的追求与探索——民主自由人权的中国实践》智库报告和纪录片。在日内瓦会场，通过现场或视频连线参会的各国外交官和专家对中国人民当家作主的伟大成就表示赞赏，对中国以人民为中心的全过程人民民主理论和实践予以高度评价。

中国常驻日内瓦代表团临时代办李松在发言中指出，当前民主成为国际上的热门话题，其中一个直接原因是个别国家企图通过召集所谓"民主峰会"开历史倒车，把世界拉回冷战时代。与此同时，这也引发国际社会回望民主的初心本意，激浊扬清，明辨是非，探讨真正的民主之道。

全人类共同价值的追求与探索 — 民主自由人权的中国实践

李松表示，在日内瓦的许多使节最近都明确表示，世界上不存在唯我独尊的民主模式，各国有权自主选择符合自身国情的政治制度和发展道路。经过最近一个时期在国际、国内诸多论坛的大思辨、大讨论，什么是真正的民主、应该由谁来定义和评判民主、民主为谁服务等等这样的问题，正在引起国际社会越来越丰富、深入的思考。

津巴布韦常驻日内瓦代表哈罗德在发言中对智库报告和纪录片的发布表示祝贺。他说，民主和人权代表的是普世的原则与目标，但应该允许各国采取不同的方式和途径。一些西方国家认为自己的模式至高无上，喜欢将自己的模式强加于别国，但历史经验证明，其后果往往只会动摇别国的稳定局面，甚至激发社会动荡。

古巴常驻日内瓦代表团参赞阿里亚斯在发言中表示，世界上没有单一的民主发展路径，各国应根据自身国情采纳相应的方式，同时不应允许某些国家将自己的模式强加于人。中国在过去几十年里为世界提供了很好的民主和人权发展范例，值得其他国家研究、借鉴。

联合国人权理事会前民主公平国际秩序问题独立专家德扎亚斯在发言中表示，民主是一种普遍价值观，其基础是人民自由表达意愿，决定自己的政治、经济、社会和文化制度并参与社会生活的各个方面。民主和人权不是世界任何一个区域的专利，而是人类的共同遗产，需要从《世界人权宣言》的高度以更加全面的方式来看待。

英国作家、社会活动家马丁内斯在发言中表示，尽管西方政客和媒体习惯于将中国刻画成非民主的形象，实际上与西方国家奉行的自由化民主相比，中国的全过程人民民主更具纯正深刻内涵，中国普通民众在社会事务中的参与度高于西方国家，而在代表普通民众的基本利益方面，中国政府做得远比西方政府更出色。

（新华社日内瓦12月7日电　记者聂晓阳、陈俊侠）

实现民主自由人权，中国做对了什么？

新华社记者

放眼世界，贫富分化、极化政治、治理失灵、国际霸凌等种种现实危机令人不安，也折射出"自由主义民主的贫困"；审视中国，社会主义民主创造了世所罕见的经济快速发展和社会长期稳定奇迹，历史性地消灭了绝对贫困，人民对生活更加美好充满信心。中国做对了什么？

新华社国家高端智库2021年12月7日向全球发布《全人类共同价值的追求与探索：民主自由人权的中国实践》报告，解码中国举世瞩目的成就背后，14亿多人追求民主、自由等全人类共同价值和人权理想所走出的道路和发现的道理，得出一系列重要发现。

——中国从民主的真谛出发，立足自身实际和文化传统，探索出人民当家作主的中国特色社会主义民主之路,"全过程人民民主"是对人类民主的守正创新。

——中国的民主路径,是以政党领导人民建立新国家,确立人民当家作主制度,开启国家现代化进程。作为"使命型政党",中国共产党的领导使亿万人民凝聚为一个有机整体,解决了落实人民主权的"超大规模民主难题"。

——民主、自由和人权的中国实践,形成了一系列行之有效的治理思想与方法,解码中国民主的"致治"之道,或可将先进政党、人民至上、聚焦发展喻为三大"关键应用"。

——中国共产党将一切政治行动都以人民整体利益为基本取向,让民主回归人民的逻辑,让自由成全人的全面发展,让幸福成为人权的最高标准,开辟了国家现代化新道路,开创了人类文明新形态。

判断制度成色的"试金石"

当代西方学者反思"自由主义民主"出现的种种问题和乱象,指出"不能回应民意的民主是无效的民主""理想的民主是选民对政治议程的最终控制",良治社会有赖于国家治理能力。

新华社国家高端智库报告指出,中国社会呈现出高"治商"特点,其标准体现为人民的安全感、获得感和幸福感,对应的是国家治理的安民、富民、乐民能力。报告从比较政治学视角,

全人类共同价值的追求与探索 —— 民主自由人权的中国实践

分析了中国民主在实现良治目标上的效能和优点。

致善政的"治理型民主"。它有三个要素，即：社会充分参与—国家自主性回应—负责任决策及其有效执行。中国的"治理型民主"不但重视政治过程的民主，更强调民主政治的结果即"良政"。

有活力的"效率型民主"。体现于治国理政各方面的民主集中制，让中国充满活力又极具执行力。它既强调充分发扬民主，激发人民的积极性主动性创造性，又重视正确地集中——在民主基础上集思广益，形成科学决策并付诸实际行动。

汇众智的"动力型民主"。坚持人民主体地位，充分调动人民积极性，被中国共产党视为立于不败之地的强大根基。没有民主，就没有今天的中国奇迹。中国梦，为中国人追求民主自由和发展人权事业描绘出崭新愿景，也将激发人民贡献自己的智慧与力量。

可检验的"系统性民主"。这体现为中国提出的"八个能否"民主标准：国家领导层能否依法有序更替，全体人民能否依法管理国家事务和社会事务、管理经济和文化事业，人民群众能否畅通表达利益要求，社会各方面能否有效参与国家政治生活，国家决策能否实现科学化、民主化，各方面人才能否通过公平竞争进入国家领导和管理体系，执政党能否依照宪法法律规定实现对国家事务的领导，权力运用能否得到有效制约和监督。

政治学者认为，"八个能否"民主标准总结了中外民主政治发展的经验教训，符合现代政治文明原则，反映了"全过程人民民主"的系统性。

落实人民主权的"新形态"

最早出现在古希腊的"民主"一词，意为"人民的统治"。现代民主以追求平等与公正为核心。"民主"的中国表达——"人民当家作主"，已经具体而现实地变成了造福14亿多人民的实践。

报告指出，"全过程人民民主"是中国民主的基本特征，它超越"少数人民主""一次性民主""伪全民性民主"，全链条、全方位、全覆盖地落实人民当家作主。

报告从"人怎么选""事怎么议""策怎么定""权怎么用"4个维度，勾勒了"全过程人民民主"在中国的运行：

不同于西方国家单纯靠选举产生的"空降兵"式的领导人，中国领导人的产生要经过一个一个政治台阶，层层选拔，出类拔萃、政绩卓著、经验丰富，才可有效治理世界上人口最多的国家。

百姓意见抵达国家最高立法机关有了"直通车"。截至2021年10月，全国人大常委会法工委基层立法联系点共就126部法律草案、年度立法计划等征求基层群众意见建议7800余条，其中2200余条被不同程度吸收采纳。

中国近年医改取得明显进展，一个重要原因是推广了地方首创经验——福建"三明模式"。在新冠肺炎疫情期间，无论武汉"封城"，还是全国驰援武汉，决策原则都是"人民至上""生命至上"。

2012年以来，中国共产党掀起史上力度空前的反腐败风暴，打"虎"无禁区，拍"蝇"不手软，猎"狐"不止步，在制度上一体推进不敢腐、不能腐、不想腐，有效遏制了腐败蔓延势头，确保人民赋予的权力用来为人民谋幸福。

实现人民当家作主的"大逻辑"

新华社国家高端智库报告从历史政治学视角指出，中国民主道路顺应历史、理论、实践和价值逻辑，坚守全人类共同价值，又立足中国大地实现了创新性发展。

报告指出，近代中国尝试过君主立宪制、议会制、多党制、总统制等多种制度模式，但都以失败告终。直到中国共产党带领人民取得新民主主义革命胜利，建立中华人民共和国，确立人民当家作主制度体系，中国才实现从几千年封建专制政治向人民民主的伟大飞跃。

报告指出，以追求者姿态踏上民主道路的新中国，力图从现代民主价值来思考和把握本国的民主路径，即马克思所揭示的民主逻辑：国家制度是人的自由的产物，国家是"人民自己的作品"。新中国民主实践的社会主义取向，意味着它是资产阶级民主的批判者和超越者。

报告指出，人民代表大会制度，落实了国家"一切权力属于人民"的宪法原则。人大代表在地域、行业、民族等结构上与整个社会的人民结构具有整体的对应性，确保国家权力机关能够全面地反映人民意愿。国家机构实行民主集中制，因而中国能形成治国理政的强大合力，切实防止出现相互掣肘、内耗严重的现象。

报告指出，良好的民主是自由和人权的基础，抓住民主建设的"牛鼻子"，人民的自由和权利就有了制度保障。新中国的建立和社会主义制度的确立，从根本上消灭了阻碍人民享有自由的旧社会制度，人民的各种权利得到宪法保障；改革开放和发展社会主义市场经济，充分激发了全社会的创造活力，顺着"改革开放—脱贫攻坚—全面小康—共同富裕"的路线图，中国人摆脱贫困过上富足而有尊严的生活。

追求全人类共同价值的"中国策"

"世界怎么了、我们怎么办？"2017年，中国国家主席习近平在联合国日内瓦总部发出时代之问。

2021年，中华人民共和国恢复联合国合法席位50周年，习近平主席给出新的思考：我们应该大力弘扬和平、发展、公平、正义、民主、自由的全人类共同价值，共同为建设一个更加美好的世界提供正确理念指引。和平与发展是我们的共同事业，公平正义是我们的共同理想，民主自由是我们的共同追求。

新华社国家高端智库报告说，追求全人类共同价值是"做正确的事"，而"把正确的事做正确"是巨大挑战，中国的民主自由人权实践，提供了有益的知识启示。

——民主如何实现善治？报告认为，先进政党、人民至上、聚焦发展或可喻为中国"致治"之道的三大"关键应用"。

作为先进政党的显著特征，中国共产党始终站在全体人民利益角度，顺应人类和时代进步的大潮流，总揽全局、协调各方，团结组织各派政治力量、各种政治资源，为全体人民谋幸福、为中华民族谋复兴。

"以人民为中心"使中国的"政道"和"治道"获得稳固价值坐标。人民拥护不拥护、赞成不赞成、高兴不高兴、答应不答应，是衡量一切工作得失的根本标准。

聚焦发展，使中国人获得了越来越多的自由和民主权利；更多的自由和民主权利，进一步促进了整个国家的发展；而发展的成效继续完善民主治理，使人民的权利得到更好保障。

——全人类共同价值如何实现？报告说，和平、发展、公平、正义、民主、自由是全人类共同价值，但其实现路径是个性化的，应该尊重不同国家人民对价值实现路径的探索。多样性不仅合乎常理，而且美好，"各美其美，美美与共"，一起向未来。

报告指出，中国民主自由和人权实践，为实现全人类共同价值提供了可以借鉴的重要原则：

实践原则：民主的有效性必须通过能否解决绝大多数人实际问题的实践来检验和完善；

自主原则：民主自由人权的路径选择必须基于本国国情，外部强加的所谓"民主改造"贻害无穷；

时序原则：促进民主、维护自由、保障人权需要循序渐进，不能超越社会发展阶段搞狂飙突进；

过程原则：民主自由人权的追求止于至善，没有最好，只有更好。

——人类怎样走向更加光明的未来？报告指出，有人曾以为，国家就是最大的政治单位，世界只是空洞的地理空间，而今天的真相是：人类是一个整体，居住的星球是一个"地球村"，任何国家都无法独善其身。

世界多极化、国际关系民主化是大势所趋，人类只有抓住历史机遇，作出正确选择，才能开创更加光明的未来。坚守全人类共同价值，构建人类命运共同体，中国为徘徊于十字路口的世界指明了正确的方向。

（新华社北京12月7日电　记者：顾钱江、梁建强、闫睿、储国强、刘丽娜、崔峰、叶书宏、郝薇薇、刘阳、宣力祺、宗巍、李怀岩、陈尚营、周蕊、刘明霞）

Countries vary in history, culture, system and economic development level, but peoples of all countries uphold the shared human values of peace, development, equity, justice, democracy and freedom.[1]

Peace and development are our common cause, equity and justice our common aspiration, and democracy and freedom our common pursuit.[2]

— Xi Jinping

---

[1] Keynote speech delivered by Xi Jinping at the Communist Party of China and World Political Parties Summit. July 6, 2021.

[2] Speech delivered by Xi Jinping at a conference marking the 50th anniversary of the restoration of the lawful seat of the People's Republic of China in the United Nations. Oct. 25, 2021.

Introduction

　　Since the founding of the People's Republic of China-- the world's most populous country and home to 56 ethnic groups-- the Communist Party of China (CPC) has led the Chinese people in creating miracles in the achievement of rapid economic growth and long-term social stability. To understand these miracles, one needs to gain a deep understanding of the economic logic behind China's policy of reform and opening-up, and the political logic behind modern China's exploration of the practice of democracy and the protection of freedom and human rights in the pursuit of the common values of humanity.

　　There is widespread familiarity with the Western

notion of democracy characterized by competitive elections between multiple parties and the separation of three powers -- executive, legislative, and judicial -- to define whether or not a country is democratic. But such methods cannot explain how China has managed to produce its two miracles for the benefit of its vast population.

The Chinese people have come to the conclusion based on experience that there is only one criterion for democratic governance: that ordinary people enjoy the dividends of peace and development and live peaceful and happy lives. The essence of modern state governance is democratic governance. Well-functioning democracy can guarantee and develop freedom and human rights.

The word "democracy," which first appeared in ancient Greece, originally meant "rule by the people." In China, "the running of the country by the people" has become a reality that is increasingly vivid and vigorous.

The Western-centric yardstick of democracy should not be the only criterion of judging good or bad governance.

Based on its own reality, China is exploring a path of inheritance and innovation in realizing democratic values and is pursuing a "substantial democracy" in which the people are the masters of the country. The democracy China practices is a "whole-process democracy" that covers all aspects and all procedures, a "governance democracy" for good governance, an "efficient democracy" with vitality, a "democracy as a driving force" with collective wisdom, and a testable "systematic democracy." All in all, it is the broadest, most genuine and most effective socialist democracy.

China has achieved remarkable results in implementing "the running of the country by the people." The success of China's democracy can be attributed to three leading features of its approach to governance: an advanced non-partisan party, people-centered philosophy, and development-focused worldview.

China is a faithful practitioner and innovator in the practice of the concepts of democracy, freedom and human rights. Although its journey is not yet complete, China's exploration has established important principles for the realization of common values of humanity:

-- Result-oriented: The effectiveness of democracy must be tested and perfected by solving the practical problems of the vast majority of people.

-- Self-determining: The path of democracy, freedom and human rights must be chosen based on national conditions, and so-called democratic transformations imposed from the outside will cause endless harm.

-- Steady-paced: To promote democracy, safeguard freedom and protect human rights, a country needs to proceed in a gradual and orderly fashion, rather than rapidly shift beyond its current stage of social development.

-- Ever-progressing: The pursuit of democracy, freedom and human rights never ends. A country should always strive for better.

With "the running of the country by the people" as its essence and characterized by a "whole-process people's democracy," China's democratic governance is constantly improving. Its criteria are whether this governance conforms to national conditions, whether it is effective, and whether it wins the support of the people. The freedom, rights and well-being of the people are also constantly increasing. Socialist democracy with Chinese characteristics has demonstrated a new form of political civilization.

Chapter I

The Running of the Country by the People: The Overarching Logic of Pursuing the Value of Democracy

"Socialist democracy with Chinese characteristics is a new thing, and a good thing."[1]

— Xi Jinping

---

[1] Speech delivered by Xi Jinping at a conference marking the 60th anniversary of the National People's Congress, Sept. 5, 2014.

How would Alexis de Tocqueville, famous for writing "Democracy in America" nearly 200 years ago, observe and reflect on the story of China today?

With a population of more than 1.4 billion, the country has eliminated absolute poverty and is forging ahead toward the goal of common prosperity for all.

It has the world's largest social security system, with basic health insurance and basic old-age insurance covering almost every Chinese.

It is the second-largest economy and the largest trader in goods in the world, contributing over 30 percent to the global economic growth every year.

Its new-energy vehicles, accounting for half of the world's total, run on the world's longest expressways.

It has the longest high-speed railway system and the most convenient express-delivery network in the world.

It has more than 1 billion netizens continuously publishing and sharing information online. It has the world's largest number of college graduates annually.

Each day, it witnesses the creation of 16,000 new enterprises and more than 120 new foreign enterprises entering the world's largest consumer market and largest investment destination.

It sees about 100 million Chinese travel abroad every year, visiting all parts of the world and returning safely.[1]

Across its more than 9.6 million square kilometers of land, 4.864 million primary-level branches of the CPC and more than 95 million CPC members actively perform their duties.[2]

A country cannot remain stable without a sound system, and a strong system contributes to a powerful country. Through China's achievements in governance featuring security, stability, growth and development in the long term, we can draw the conclusion that a vigorous democracy -- socialist democracy with Chinese characteristics -- has become a reality benefiting more than 1.4 billion people. This democratic path conforms to the logic of history, theory, practice and value, adheres to the common values of

---

[1] Some of the data above are taken from the speech delivered by Chinese Ambassador to the United States Qin Gang in a conversation jointly held by the Carter Center and the George H.W. Bush Foundation for U.S.-China Relations, official website of Embassy of the People's Republic of China in the United States of America, September. 22, 2021.
http://www.china-embassy.org/dshd/202109/t20210923_9594567.htm

[2] Statistical Bulletin of the Communist Party of China, Xinhuanet, June 30, 2021. http://www.xinhuanet.com/politics/2021-06/30/c_1127611673.htm

humanity, and has achieved innovative development based on China's conditions.

1.1 Logic of History: The People's Choice

The democratic path, which ensures that the country is run by the people, is chosen by the Chinese people historically.

-- The Road to Democracy

In 2021, a hit TV series "The Age of Awakening" brought the Chinese back to a historical scene over a hundred years ago: Faced with the tragic reality of a country enduring incessant foreign invasions and its people leading a life of extreme destitution, advanced Chinese intellectuals launched the New Culture Movement and called for saving China with democracy and science, thus leading to the founding of the CPC in 1921. This party, which struggled for the toiling masses, held high the banner of democracy and led the people to establish the People's Republic of China in 1949, which marked the victory of the New Democratic Revolution, and the country's great transformation from a

Chapter I The Running of the Country by the People: The Overarching Logic of Pursuing the Value of Democracy

millennia-old feudal autocracy to a people's democracy.[1]

The facts above reveal the democratic path chosen by the Party and the Chinese people: The Party led the Chinese to found the People's Republic of China, ensured the position of the people as masters of the country and launched the country's process of modernization.

To understand this model, we must first understand the CPC. It is a "mission-driven political party," whose original aspiration and mission is to seek happiness for the people and rejuvenation for the nation. It is a "people's party," which is born for the people and successful because of the people. In leading and relying on the people to advance the revolution and found New China, it has become the vanguard and leading core trusted by the people.

A hundred years ago, the Communist Party of China was founded, with the goal of making the country stronger and people richer as well as seeking happiness for the people and rejuvenation for the nation. Over the past 100

---

[1] The Resolution On Major Achievements And Historical Experience of the Party Over The Past Century, adopted at the sixth plenary session of the 19th CPC Central Committee.

years, the original aspiration and the mission of the CPC has never changed.

In the past eight years, the Party has led the people to win the fight against poverty, with nearly 100 million people living in rural areas lifted out of absolute poverty. To achieve this arduous task, China sent 255,000 work teams to the villages, more than 3 million Party first secretaries and village-stationed officials fought on the battlefield of poverty, and more than 1,800 of those officials sacrificed their lives in the line of duty.[1]

CPC Members Devoted to Fight Against COVID-19 and Poverty

Since the Covid-19 outbreak, close to **400** Party members and officials have lost their lives in the line of duty.

More than **1,800** Party members and officials also gave their lives in the battle against absolute poverty.

Source: The CPC: Its Mission and Contributions

---

[1] Statistics are from the speech at the National Conference to Review the Fight Against Poverty and Commend Individuals and Groups Involved delivered by Xi Jinping, February 25, 2021.

Chapter I The Running of the Country by the People: The Overarching Logic of Pursuing the Value of Democracy

The legitimacy of the CPC is derived from history and is determined by people's hearts and minds. It is the choice of the people. The Party knows better than any other that gaining this position does not mean that it can henceforth rest on its laurels. Therefore, it repeatedly admonishes all members that maintaining close ties with the people is the Party's "biggest advantage," and distance from the people the "biggest danger."

-- Avoiding History's Cycle

Chinese history has witnessed the sudden rise and fall of past dynasties.[1] In 1945, Mao Zedong replied to visiting democratic personages in a cave home in Yan'an: We have found a new path, and we can break free from this cycle and the new path is democracy.[2]

The key question is, what kind of democracy?

---

[1] From "Chronicle of Zuo", a commentary to the Spring and Autumn Annals, a chronicle ascribed to Confucius.

[2] Building the Cornerstone of Democracy for National Rejuvenation —A Review of China's Whole-process Democracy Developed by the Communist Party of China Central Committee with Comrade Xi Jinping as the Core, Xinhuanet, October 12, 2021. http://www.news.cn/2021-10/12/c_1127948849.htm

Regarding the choice of political systems, modern China has tried various models such as constitutional monarchy, a parliamentary system, a multi-party system, and a presidential government, but they all ended in failure. In September 1949, when the birth of New China was in sight, the First Plenary Session of the Chinese People's Political Consultative Conference reached a consensus on the political system of the new country, that is, making the National People's Congress the highest organ of state power. When the National People's Congress is not in session, the Central People's Government is the highest organ exercising state power. Governments at all levels should adopt the system of democratic centralism.[1] In 1954, the First Session of the First National People's Congress (NPC) of New China was convened, which adopted the country's first Constitution, and established China's system for governance, with a system of people's congresses as the fundamental political system.

"The system of people's congresses ensures that all

---

[1] A Brief History of the People's Republic of China, published by People's Publishing House, Contemporary China Publishing House, 2021, P6.

Chapter I The Running of the Country by the People: The Overarching Logic of Pursuing the Value of Democracy

power in the country belongs to the people; ensures that the country is run by the people to the fullest extent; upholds the unity of Party leadership, the running of the country by the people, and law-based governance; effectively guarantees that our national governance can avoid the cycles of history," said Chinese President Xi Jinping in 2021 when reviewing the 67-year history of people's congresses.[1]

> **Column: China's people's congresses**
>
> The Chinese Constitution stipulates that all power in the country belongs to the people. The people not only have the right to vote but also have the right to widely participate in governance according to the law. In China, the NPC and local people's congresses at various levels are the organs through which the people exercise state power, with the NPC being the supreme body of state power. China's NPC is also a member of the Inter-Parliamentary Union, the world's most influential parliamentary organization.

---

[1] An important speech delivered by Xi Jinping at a central conference on work related to people's congresses, Xinhuanet, October 14, 2021. http://www.news.cn/politics/leaders/2021-10/14/c_1127956955.htm

At the same time, China's people's congresses are also very different from the parliaments of Western countries. For example, unlike Western parliaments, there is no parliamentary party group in the people's congresses, and seats in the people's congresses are not allocated according to parties. Deputies to the National People's Congress, whether CPC members or members from other political parties or personages without party affiliation, all shoulder the expectations of the people and perform their duties for the people in accordance with the law.

Direct elections are conducted for deputies to the people's congresses at the county and township levels in China, and indirect elections are held above the county level. The people can elect their representatives to participate in the deliberation and administration of state affairs as well as to elect leading members of state organs. Deputies to the people's congresses have close ties with the masses. All major legislative decisions in China are made in accordance with procedures, through democratic deliberation, and through scientific and democratic decision-making.

In the practice of the NPC, it is rare to veto a resolution. Perhaps some people will think that the National People's Congress is not so important. However, the fact is that there will be a very thorough discussion before the vote, and good suggestions will be adopted.

> Finally, when deputies enter the great hall to vote, their concerns and opinions have already been taken into account and absorbed into a more well-rounded version of the text. Of course, there will always be negative votes and abstentions, which are normal practices.
>
> Source: the website of the NPC and Qin Gang, Fu Ying's introduction to the National People's Congress system

1.2 Theoretical Logic: The Work of the People

After the draft of the first Constitution of New China was made public in June 1954, about a quarter of the country's population, or 150 million people, participated in the discussion and put forward more than 1.18 million opinions.[1]

This unanimously adopted constitution is known as "the people's constitution," and "all state power belongs to the people"; the country's name includes "people"; the organs of state power are the people's congresses, and governments at all levels are the "people's governments." Defining the country's system in the name of "the people" signifies that

---

[1] Material from the Museum of the 1954 Constitution in Hangzhou, Zhejiang

the people are placed at the moral high ground, and the government must be accountable to the people.

-- Grasping the Essence of Democracy

Slogans of the Western bourgeois revolutions, such as freedom and democracy, were exciting, but only a fraction of people's democracy had actually been achieved. It was not until the rise of vigorous labor movements in the middle of the 19th century, after the resolute efforts of the masses, had mass democracy - with the pursuit of equality and justice as its core - gradually become a modern trend sweeping across the world and a common value of humanity.[1] The Chinese democratic practice of "the running of the country by the people" is part of this global trend.

New China, which embarked on the road of democracy as a pursuer, tried to grasp a democratic path of its own from the values of modern democracy, that is, the logic of democracy as revealed by Karl Marx: the state system is the product of human freedom, and the people are not

---

[1] Yang Guangbin: *The Dimension of Democratic Socialism -- Comments on the myth of the bourgeoisie and democratic politics*, Social Sciences in China, 2009.

Chapter I The Running of the Country by the People: The Overarching Logic of Pursuing the Value of Democracy

the work of the state. On the contrary, the country is "the people's own work." The people become the masters of the country. The goal of the country is to maximize the free and comprehensive development of the people.[1]

The socialist orientation of New China's democratic practice means that it is a critic of and transcends bourgeois democracy. The people's sovereignty to be realized -- "the running of the country by the people" -- is a broad, genuine, and effective democracy. It is a people-centered democracy, not capital-oriented democracy.

-- Taking root in China

The adaptation of Marxism to the Chinese context -- adapting the basic tenets of Marxism to China's specific realities and China's fine traditional culture -- is the theoretical code for the Communist Party of China to lead the people from standing up and growing prosperous, to becoming strong. Similarly, democracy can only flourish

---

[1] Lin Shangli: *The People, Political Parties and the State: Political Analysis of the Development of People's Democracy*, Fudan Journal (Social Sciences Edition), 2011.

when it is deeply rooted in Chinese soil.

China's democratic development combines the "goal-oriented" realization of people's happiness, national prosperity and national rejuvenation, the "reality" on the ground of the world's most populous developing country, and the "historical dimension" of a history of 5,000 years of civilization. By remembering its roots, absorbing outside ideas, facing the future, continuous integration, summarizing, refining and sublimating, China has formed a new form of democracy.

Through long-term socialist practice, China has deeply realized that "poverty is not socialism" and that "people's democracy is the lifeblood of socialism."

1.3 Logic in Practice: Initiative in Institutional Design

Shen Jilan, a woman from a humble background in rural Shanxi Province, witnessed the beginning of the people's congress system in China.

In September 1954, 25-year-old Shen made her way from her home in mountainous Shanxi to Beijing for the first session of the NPC as a lawmaker chosen through a democratic election. Her journey was difficult. She first rode a donkey, then a bus and took several train rides before arriving in Beijing. Through her initiative, women in rural cooperatives gained the right to equal pay for equal work. The first Constitution of the People's Republic of China, which Shen voted for, stipulates, "Women in the People's Republic of China shall enjoy equal rights with men in all spheres of life: political, economic, cultural, social and familial."

In June 2020, Shen died at the age of 91. She served as a national lawmaker at 13 consecutive NPC sessions and spoke up for the people throughout her life. Her story reflects the essence of the people's congress system.

Protecting women's rights to participation in the administration of public affairs

The 13th NPC has 742 female deputies accounting for 24.9 percent of the total

12.9 percentage points higher than the figure for the First NPC in 1954

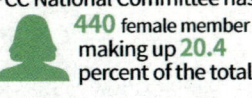

The 13th CPPCC National Committee has 440 female member making up 20.4 percent of the total

14.3 percentage points higher than that for the First CPPCC National Committee in 1949

Source: Seeking Happiness for People: 70 Years of Progress on Human Rights in China

-- Broad Representation

The people's congress system puts into action the constitutional principle of "all power in the People's Republic of China belongs to the people." The general public elects deputies who represent their will and interests to form organs of state power at various levels. The NPC is the highest state organ of power.

Broad representation is the hallmark of the system. Currently, there are more than 2.6 million deputies to people's congresses at various levels. They proportionately come from different regions, trades and ethnic groups, ensuring that organs of state power fully represent the will of the people. In the current NPC, 15.7 percent of the deputies exercise state power on behalf of workers and farmers, and 55 ethnic minority groups have deputies from their respective ethnic groups.[1]

---

[1] State Council Information Office: white paper titled "The Communist Party of China and Human Rights Protection - A 100-Year Quest" released in June 2021. http://www.scio.gov.cn/zfbps/32832/Document/1707301/1707301.htm

Percentage of deputies and members from ethnic minority groups

Source: The Communist Party of China and Human Rights Protection – A 100-Year Quest

Deputies to people's congresses do not work as full-time lawmakers but have their own jobs and careers. Many of them work in primary-level positions.[1] The logic behind this is to stay connected with the people. With this approach, deputies to people's congresses could better play their role of connecting with the people so that legislation will better reflect the will of the people, pool wisdom from the people and deliver benefits to the people.

---

[1] The Law of the People's Republic of China on Deputies to the National People's Congress and to the Local People's Congresses at Various Levels, official website of the National People's Congress, http://www.npc.gov.cn/npc/c12488/201508/87e9a47af39c4480b952e1ab76b8e9cb.shtml.

Shen's story serves as a case in point for democracy and is a victory for women's rights. Chai Shanshan, a deliveryman serving as a lawmaker, has personal experience indicative of how China's democracy has evolved with the times. One of the millions of Chinese working in the country's booming courier service sector, Chai was elected deputy to the NPC in 2018. At the fourth session of the 13th NPC held in 2021, he drafted proposals including one on improving social security for workers on flexible jobs in sectors like ride hailing, courier service and food delivery, which directly prompted legislation in this regard.

-- Democratic Centralism

China's Constitution stipulates, "The state institutions of the People's Republic of China shall practice the principle of democratic centralism." The NPC and the local people's congresses at all levels shall be created through a democratic election and shall be accountable to the people and subject to their oversight. All administrative, supervisory, adjudicatory and procuratorial organs of the state shall be created by the people's congresses and shall be accountable to them and subject to their oversight.[1] Under the Party's leadership, organs of state power constitute an integral body, in which the organs of state power have their respective functions but act in coordination, fully uphold democracy and effectively exercise centralism. The arrangement leaves no room for talkfests, decisions without execution, or execution of decisions without concrete outcomes.[2]

Democratic centralism is a principle as well as a method, meaning that by fully practicing democracy, the right decisions are thereby reached and rigorously implemented. For this reason, the system of people's congresses has created a powerful synergy in governing the country, so that different state organs do not hold each other back or waste energy on quibbling with each other. It has provided an important institutional guarantee for the CPC to lead the people in creating the miracle of rapid economic growth and long-term social stability.

---

[1] Constitution of the People's Republic of China, People's Publishing House, March 2018, P8.
[2] Xi Jinping: On Upholding the System of Running of the Country by the People, Central Party Literature Press, 2021, P277.

After a long period of practice, Chinese leaders have come to the conclusion that the system of people's congresses is "a great creation in the history of human political systems and a brand-new political system of great significance in the history of political development in China and even in the world".[1]

-- The Party-People-Law Synergy

The CPC has not only accomplished its mission of establishing the People's Republic of China, but also taken up the challenge of large-scale democracy after it came to power: how to make hundreds of millions of people become one whole and ensure that the state power is in the hands of the people?

China has found the answer in practice – to generate synergic interaction of Party leadership, the running of the country by the people, and law-based governance. The Party leadership answers the question of "who shall

---

[1] Speech by Xi Jinping at a central conference on work related to people's congresses, xinhuanet.com, Oct. 14, 2021.
http://www.news.cn/politics/leaders/2021-10/14/c_1127956955.htm

unite the people," the running of the country by the people answers "what is the purpose of democracy," and law-based governance answers "how to govern the country."

The inherent mechanism involves the following aspects: the people, under the CPC's leadership, unite as an organic whole; the common will of the Party and the people is embodied in the Constitution and the law; the state is organized, run and developed with the Constitution as the fundamental law; power must be exercised within the framework of the rule of law; the people, with the CPC at the core, manage state, economic, cultural and social affairs through various ways and forms in accordance with the law; and the Constitution and law and their enforcement must reflect the will of the people, protect the people's rights and interests and spur their creativity.

-- Institutional Framework for the Running of the Country by the People

The very design of the democratic institutions of New China incorporates foresight to prevent chaos.

The system of CPC-led multi-party cooperation and political consultation aims to strengthen the cooperation and coordination of various social forces and avoid factional strife between different political parties. The system of regional ethnic autonomy aims to forge a strong sense of community among the Chinese people and guard against estrangement and conflict between ethnic groups. The system of community-level self-governance aims to ensure that the people directly exercise their democratic rights in accordance with the law and prevent the emergence of a situation in which the people have nominal but not real power.

The three "basic political systems," together with "the fundamental political system" of people's congresses, underpin the institutional framework for the running of the country by the people.

-- "Two Wheels" of Election and Consultation

Some describe Chinese democracy as "running on two wheels," namely electoral democracy in which people exercise their right to vote in elections and consultative democracy in which people from all sectors of society undertake extensive deliberations and reach consensus on common issues before major decisions are made. These two forms of democratic setting greatly improve the efficacy of democracy as they play their respective roles at different levels and in different areas while being complementary to each other. The annual "two sessions" of the National People's Congress and the National Committee of the Chinese People's Political Consultative Conference are seen as prolonged "democracy open days" where people witness the robust performance of the "two wheels" of Chinese democracy.

The essence of the people's democracy lies in reaching a consensus on the aspirations and needs of the whole society by enabling the people to discuss their own affairs. "Consultative democracy," which originates from the CPC's practice in the old revolutionary base of Shaanxi Province more than 80 years ago, is a distinctive feature of China's socialist democracy that fully embodies this spirit.

An important aim of the current reform of China's political system is to promote an extensive, multi-level, and institutionalized development of consultative democracy. In China, new policies have been smoothly introduced because a large number of conflicts and demands have been resolved or absorbed beforehand in the consultation process.

1.4 Logic in values: Emancipating the People

Karl Marx said that only through true democracy can humankind achieve complete emancipation. An ideal Communist society in Marx's vision was defined as "an association in which the free development of each is the condition for the free development of all."

Marx defined "human emancipation" as "the free development of each," and the "free development" of human beings was upheld as the most important democratic value. Based on Marx's understanding, a democratic political system that ensures the people run the country is the prerequisite for realizing the value of freedom.

Column: Democracy, Freedom and Human Rights in China's Constitution

The current version of China's Constitution makes 14 references to "democracy," 13 to "freedom," and 31 to "human rights" and "rights."

In regards to democracy, New Democratic Revolution, socialist democracy, people's democratic dictatorship, democratic centralism and democratic management, among other terms, are mentioned in the general principles of the Constitution.

In regards to freedom, Article 4 of the Constitution provides that all ethnic groups shall have the freedom to use and develop their own spoken and written languages and to preserve or reform their own traditions and customs. According to Chapter II, where the Constitution stipulates the fundamental rights and obligations of citizens, all citizens shall enjoy various kinds of freedom, including freedom of speech, the press, assembly, association, procession and demonstration, freedom of religious belief, personal freedom, freedom of correspondence, freedom to engage in cultural activities and freedom of marriage.

In regards to human rights, Article 33 of the Constitution provides that the state shall respect and protect human rights. A total of nine articles refer to the protection of civil rights, such as property rights, the right to work and rest, the right to receive education, and the rights of women, all ethnic groups, foreigners in the territory of China and Chinese nationals overseas.

Source: Constitution of the People's Republic of China amended in March 2018.

It had been made clear to the Chinese people that, from years of suffering from the Opium War in 1840 to the founding of the People's Republic of China in 1949, there would be no true freedom and human rights without national independence and liberation. The founding of New China and the establishment of a socialist system had crushed the old social system that stood in the way of people's access to freedom, bringing various rights of the people under the protection of the Constitution. Through the reform and opening up and the development of a socialist market economy, society's creativity has been fully unleashed, the economy has maintained rapid growth on a long-term basis, and the Chinese people have led more prosperous lives. Entering a new era, China, in a historic move, has put an end to absolute poverty and ushered in moderate prosperity in all respects for a population of over 1.4 billion. Seeing their aspirations for a better life become a reality, the Chinese people now enjoy greater confidence, independence and strength.

"Freedom means having an environment that allows you to achieve your goals," said world-renowned trend watcher

Chapter I The Running of the Country by the People: The Overarching Logic of Pursuing the Value of Democracy

John Naisbitt in his observations on China.[1]

The pursuit of democracy, freedom and human rights also serves as the driving force behind China's development and prosperity. Following the roadmap of reform and opening up – poverty eradication – moderate prosperity – common prosperity, the Chinese people have shaken off poverty and live well-off lives with dignity because of the firm implementation of a people's democracy.

China's Achievements in Poverty Alleviation

China's fight against poverty entered a critical stage after the 18th CPC National Congress in 2012. At the end of 2020, through eight years of hard work, China achieved the goal of eliminating extreme poverty. The **98.99 million** people in rural areas who were living below the current poverty threshold all shook off poverty.

All the 832 designated poor counties and **128,000** impoverished villages got rid of poverty.

China has eliminated poverty over entire regions. ✓

 Since reform and opening-up, more than **770 million** of China's rural population living below the current poverty line have been raised from poverty

accounting for more than **70** percent of the global total over the same period according to the World Bank's international poverty standard

Source: Poverty Alleviation: China's Experience and Contribution

---

[1] John Naisbitt&Doris Naisbitt: *China's Megatrends: The 8 Pillars of a New Society*, Jilin Publishing Group, September, 2009, P176.

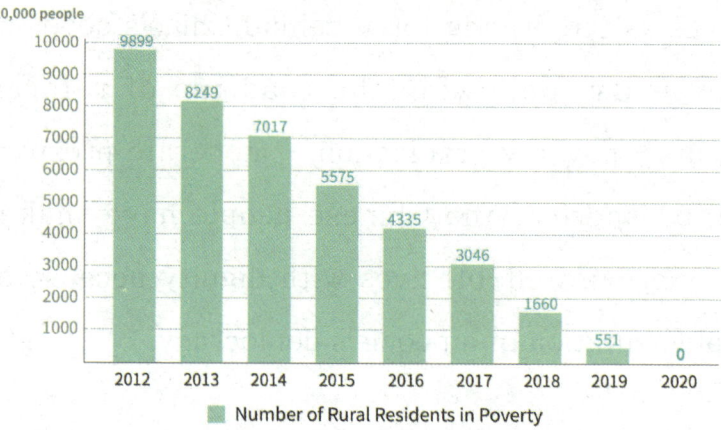

Chapter II

Whole-process Democracy: a New Form of Implementing People's Sovereignty

If the people are awakened only at the time of voting but go dormant soon after, if they listen to slogans at the time of the election but have no say after the election, or if they are favored at the time of canvassing but are left out in the cold after the election, such a democracy is not a true democracy.[1]

— Xi Jinping

---

[1] http://www.news.cn/politics/leaders/2021-10/14/c_1127956955.htm

Democracy means that the people are the masters of their country. They participate in and manage the affairs of their country and society. The Chinese people have the right to participate extensively in state governance, a right which is embodied in all aspects of China's democratic elections, democratic consultations, democratic decision-making, democratic management and democratic supervision.

"Whole-process democracy" pursues the unification of process and results-based democracy, procedural democracy and substantive democracy, direct democracy and indirect democracy, as well as people's democracy and state will. "Whole-process democracy" can be described in four areas: electing officials, deliberating state affairs, making policies, and overseeing the use of power.

2.1 How Does China Select Officials?

Capable state leaders and officials at all levels are necessary to run a country with a territory as vast and a population as large as China.[1] In the Chinese mechanism of selecting officials, moral integrity, professional ability and past governing performances are the basic requirements for selection involving a democratic election to determine qualified officials. Canadian political scholar Daniel A. Bell noted that the meritocracy that has existed in Chinese politics since ancient times laid the cultural underpinning of China's modern official selection system.[2]

-- Pyramids for Official Promotion

Studies have found that Chinese cadres often begin their careers at the primary level, and are promoted step by step through the township level, county level and prefecture level before becoming high-ranking provincial or ministerial-level officials. Among the over 7 million Chinese cadres, only one in 14,000 will be promoted to the executive ministerial level. On average, it takes 23 years to earn a senior position.[3]

---

[1] https://www.guancha.cn/HuAnGang/2017_10_24_432019.shtml
[2] Daniel A. Bell: *The China Model: Political Meritocracy and the Limits of Democracy*, CITIC Press Group, September, 2016.
[3] http://jingji.cntv.cn/special/wlznldz/bhy/39/index.shtml

Unlike leaders in Western countries, who can often assume their offices through elections alone, Chinese statespeople are selected through multiple tests. Only cadres with outstanding achievements and adequate experience are qualified to undertake important roles in China's governance.

The CPC focuses more on selecting competitive cadres than any other political organization around the world, said Eric Li, a venture capitalist and political scientist.[1] The CPC's elite group maintains high mobility, noted Cheng Li, director of the John L. Thornton China Center at the Brookings Institution. He said that more than 60 percent of the members of the recent CPC Central Committees, with a term of five years, have been new faces.[2] Such high mobility in an elite political group is rare around the world, and it ensures the competitiveness and optimization of democratic governance.

---

[1] Eric Li: The Great Power of Chinese Democracy, People's Daily, April 1, 2013.

[2] Yuan Jing: The Mechanism of Power Balance and Anti-corruption in China: Interview with Li Cheng, director of the John L. Thornton China Center of the Brookings Institution, People's Tribune, Volume 12, 2014

-- 94 Percent of People's Congress Deputies are Directly Elected

It's rarely known that the overwhelming majority of Chinese grassroots public representatives (equivalent to councilors) are directly elected. The first constitution of the People's Republic of China promulgated in 1954 endowed Chinese citizens with universal and equal suffrage, and more than 99 percent of adult Chinese citizens had the right to vote and stand for election. By then, many other countries still restricted voting rights based on race, gender, and other factors.

As of April 2021, deputies to people's congresses at all five levels, including the state and township levels, exceeded 2.62 million. Of the total, 94 percent were from the county and township levels, all directly elected on a one-person-one-vote basis.[1]

Giving play to the role of deputies to people's congresses at all levels is a significant manifestation of people being

---

[1] Zhang Yesui, spokesperson for the fourth session of the 13th National People's Congress, answered Chinese and foreign reporters' questions at a press conference of the session. http://www.gov.cn/xinwen/2021-03/05/content_5590356.htm

masters of the country. Those deputies must give full play to the principal role of a whole-process people's democracy. That means the deputies should constantly enrich the vehicles of connections with the people to maintain close ties and better reflect social conditions and public opinion.

2.2 How do People Participate in Public Affairs Deliberations?

The whole-process people's democracy emphasizes citizen participation in the whole process of public policy making. This allows citizens to participate before, during, and after the decision-making, and safeguards people's right to be informed, participate, be heard and oversee in order to find the best solution while drawing on the pooled wisdom of the people.

-- Local Legislative Outreach offices

As of April 2021, the national legislature has publicly solicited opinions on draft laws on 230 occasions. In recent years, the Commission of Legislative Affairs of the National People's Congress Standing Committee set up local legislative outreach offices, which offered a direct channel for grassroots opinions to reach the highest legislature of the country. As of October 2021, 22 outreach offices nationwide had put forward more than 7,800 opinions and suggestions for 126 draft laws and annual legislative plans, over 2,200 of which were absorbed and adopted to varying degrees, creating a more refined legislation process.[1]

One of the opinions was from Li Junhao, a high school student from Shanghai. In August 2020, relevant parties visited the high school, affiliated with East China University of Political Science and Law, to solicit opinions on the revised draft of the Law on the Protection of Minors. Li put forward a suggestion -- "The economic conditions of each minor's family are different. If the guardian who has committed domestic violence against the minor refuses to accept family education guidance, the guardian is to be punished with the confiscation of the security deposit. This will worsen the situation of families." His suggestion was

---

[1] Building Bridges to Connect the People and the Highest Legislature -- Roundup of the Work of Local Legislative Outreach Offices of the Commission of Legislative Affairs of the National People's Congress Standing Committee, xinhuanet.com, Nov.2, 2021. https://baijiahao.baidu.com/s?id=1715313995789558909&wfr=spider&for=pc

adopted by the Standing Committee of the National People's Congress. The newly-revised law was passed, removing the requirement from the draft that the guardians of minors pay a security deposit.

China's process to solicit proposals from the public

Since the 18th CPC National Congress, central committees of the other political parties and non-affiliates have submitted more than **730** proposals to the CPC Central Committee and the State Council From the First Session of the 13th CPPCC National Committee held in March 2018 to April 2021, the CPPCC National Committee received **23,048** proposals.

 By April 2021, the state legislatures had solicited public opinion on **230** draft laws.

 A total of **425,762** comments were received for the draft Civil Code alone, collecting **1,021,834** pieces of opinion.

Sources: The Communist Party of China and Human Rights Protection – A 100-Year Quest

-- Democratic Discussion

Originated in Wenling, Zhejiang Province, in 1999, "democratic discussion" is a type of "grassroots democracy" that manages public affairs through full consultations. Local people review the public budget and employees of enterprises negotiate their salaries through discussion. Such discussions have become a necessity for the township government when making major decisions. "When there is a conflict, a democratic discussion is held." This model of handling related affairs has become habitual for Wenling locals.

In fact, various forms of grassroots consultative democracy created in local areas play a vital role in realizing good governance in China. Examples include the "township counselors' meeting" in Deqing, Zhejiang Province; the "Gubei citizens' council" in the Changning district, Shanghai; the "night talk" in Ganzhou, Jiangxi Province; and the "'2+4' grassroots governance" in the Changle community in Xi'an, Shaanxi Province.

2.3 How are Policies Made?

For a long time, China's reform has been referred to as "crossing the river by feeling the stones." But what is fascinating to uncover is why China has so often been able to feel the "stones" correctly. It reflects the scientific nature of policy-making in China's democratic governance. For example, outlines of the five-year plan for national economic and social development and other policies well illustrate democratic decision-making procedures.

Moreover, with full respect for the pioneering spirit seen at the grassroots level, the central government applies valuable grassroots experience in the decision-making of national reforms. The central government also first tests out major national reform measures at the regional level to gain experience before expanding them nationwide.

-- Target Management

Chinese administrators are good at planning, and managing goals and expectations.

Since the founding of the People's Republic of China, China has prepared and implemented 14 five-year plans. "The Party puts forward suggestions, the government drafts plans, the National People's Congress deliberates and approves plans, and the whole country implements the plans, creating an overall positive experience created by the CPC in state governance."[1]

---

[1] What Makes the Fifth Plenary Session of the 19th CPC Central Committee So Important and Special? -- An Exclusive Interview with Li Junru, Former Vice President of the Party School of the CPC Central Committee, www.chinanews.com, Oct. 25, 2020.
https://www.chinanews.com.cn/gn/2020/10-25/9321975.shtml

-- Grassroots Experience

Medical reform is an enduring problem across the world. China, with a population of more than 1.4 billion, has made remarkable progress in medical reforms in recent years, and one of the important reasons is that it has popularized the local pioneering experience -- "the Sanming Model." Thanks to the interconnectedness of medicine, medical insurance, and medical treatment in Sanming, Fujian Province, the problem of "difficult and expensive medical treatment" has been effectively resolved. Based on Sanming's good practice, China set up the National Healthcare Security Administration, carried out collective procurement, and reduced the prices of medicines and consumables considerably, much to the satisfaction of the local population. After the central government put forward the new goal of a "Healthy China," Sanming actively worked with local hospitals to shift from treating diseases to focusing on overall health in its medical reforms. The experience was once again affirmed by the central government and promoted across entire country.

-- Decision-making in the Fight Against COVID-19

In some cases, decision-making is an extremely difficult process. One example is the decision of the Chinese leadership to lock down the city of Wuhan, Hubei Province, when the COVID-19 epidemic broke out at the beginning of 2020. To stop the epidemic from spreading to the whole country, it was necessary to control the flow of people into and out of the city, home to over 10 million residents. At the same time, the central government mobilized the whole nation to support Wuhan and Hubei and carry out an unprecedented rescue operation. Not long after that, the epidemic situation in Wuhan and Hubei, and the whole country, was effectively brought under control, achieving a breathtaking victory in epidemic prevention and control.

Whether the lockdown of Wuhan or its rescue, the principles of decision-making were always "people first" and "life first." Under the epidemic, the people of Wuhan made a significant contribution to the national fight against the epidemic with their commitment to "protecting a nation by locking down a city," while the people of the country supported Wuhan, quickly contained the epidemic, and saved lives so that the city restarted and restored its vitality as soon as possible. Witnessing how the Chinese people have balanced collective freedom and individual freedom, Japanese director Ryo Takeuchi, who produced the documentary "Long Time No See Wuhan," exclaimed: "China's success in controlling the epidemic and restoring its economy at the same time is the result of the joint efforts of its more than 1.4 billion people."

2.4 How is "Power" Exercised?

Power without supervision is bound to produce corruption. Power is a "double-edged sword." Exercising power by the law can benefit the people, while the illegal and unlawful exercise of power is bound to harm the country and the people. China uses a series of institutional arrangements such as intraparty oversight, oversight by the National People's Congress, democratic oversight, administrative oversight, judicial oversight, public oversight, and oversight through public opinion to set up, regulate, restrain, and oversee the exercise of power by law. These measures ensure that power is exercised within an institutional cage.

-- The "Goldbach's Conjecture" of State Governance

The CPC has compared self-monitoring to the Goldbach Conjecture of State Governance, and one of the strategic arrangements for institutional innovation to solve this problem is "inspection." The central government sends inspection teams to lower-level departments, giving them the authority to independently monitor and investigate. This mechanism strengthens political inspections and identifies problems, focusing on six aspects such as the Party's political, ideological and organizational conduct and discipline and the task of securing an overwhelming victory in fighting corruption. The top-down organizational supervision and the bottom-up supervision of the masses are effectively combined, which is more conducive to finding problems and exerting a deterrent effect.

-- Oversight by Non-CPC Political Parties

Democratic oversight in China is multidimensional. It is a particular form related to China's new model of political party system. Under this system, the CPC works in cooperation with eight non-CPC political parties, among others. Non-CPC political parties are not opposition parties but parties that participate in state governance and are regarded by the CPC as "friends with admonitions" -- true friends who can offer frank criticism and suggestions.

Since 2016, the central committees of China's non-CPC political parties have launched a "democratic oversight over poverty alleviation" initiative in eight central and western provincial-level regions with large, poorer populations and high poverty incidences, respectively. It was the first time China's democratic parties carried out such supervision over the implementation of major national strategies. Having put forward more than 2,400 comments, criticisms, and advice to these provinces and more than 80 reports to the CPC Central Committee and the State Council, the initiative played a significant role in securing a victory in the battle against poverty.[1]

-- A New Model of Oversight on State Power

"If we let a few hundred corrupt officials slip through the cracks, we would let down all 1.3 billion Chinese

---

[1] The State Council Information Office, white paper titled China's Political Party System: Cooperation and Consultation, June 2021.
http://www.scio.gov.cn/zfbps/ndhf/44691/Document/1707421/1707421.htm

people."[1] Based on this recognition, since 2012, the CPC launched an unprecedented anti-corruption campaign, striking "tigers" (high-ranking offenders) without limit, swatting "flies" (low-level corrupt officials) without hesitation, and hunting down "foxes" (corrupt fugitives) without stopping. By making government employees not dare, not able to, and not want to commit corruption through institutional arrangements, the CPC has effectively curbed the corruption from spreading.

With the establishment of the National Supervisory Commission and promulgation of the Supervision Law in 2018, China has launched a new model of oversight on state power. It covers all Party members and public officials exercising public power, fundamentally shaping a standardized and sound anti-corruption system.

Through more than 70 years of exploration and practice, China has developed a broad, genuine and effective democracy and embarked on a path of democratic development suited to its national conditions.

---

[1] A speech by Xi Jinping at the fifth plenary session of the 18th Central Commission for Discipline Inspection (CCDI) of the CPC on Jan.13, 2015.

> **Column: China's View of Democracy**
>
> China's view of democracy positions the people as masters of the country. The "whole-process people's democracy" is a fundamental feature of China's democracy, an all-dimensional, democracy with a complete set of institutions, and the broadest, most genuine, and most effective socialist democracy.
>
> This democracy adheres to a people-centered approach. It transcends "democracy for the few," "one-time democracy," and "pseudo-universal democracy," ensuring that the broad masses of the people enjoy democratic rights and democratic achievements and that the concept of democracy is deeply rooted in people's minds.

Chapter III

A Democracy that Works: a Touchstone for Testing Institutional Effectiveness

"Whether a country's path of development works is judged first and foremost by whether it fits the country's conditions. Whether it follows the development trend of the times, whether it brings about economic growth, social advancement, better livelihoods, and social stability, whether it has the people's endorsement and support, and whether it contributes to the progressive cause of humanity."[1]

— Xi Jinping

---

[1] Chinese President Xi Jinping's remarks at the conference marking the 50th anniversary of the restoration of People's Republic of China's lawful seat in UN, Oct. 25, 2021.

Chapter III A Democracy that Works: a Touchstone for Testing Institutional Effectiveness

"It is not what is said but what is done that matters." The saying reflects Chinese pragmatism. In this sense, democracy must be real and effective. If it cannot translate into good governance and benefit the people, it must be viewed with suspicion no matter how attractive it looks.

3.1 "Governance Democracy" for Good Governance

According to a poll jointly released by Alliance of Democracies, Rasmussen Global and the German institute Dalia Research in June 2020, 84 percent of the Chinese respondents viewed democracy as important, and 73 percent of them believed that China is a democratic country, the sixth-highest proportion among all 53 countries and regions surveyed. China also ranked second on the government serving the majority of its people.[1]

The poll results have justified the conclusions of several observers: for the Chinese people, democracy

---

[1] Democracy Perception Index 2020, Alliance of Democracies, Rasmussen Global, and Dalia Research, June 2021.
https://www.allianceofdemocracies.org/initiatives/the-copenhagen-democracy-summit/dpi-2020/

means that the government, in the process of decision-making, should always keep in mind the interests of the overwhelming majority of the people, solicit and listen to the opinions of the people, and serve the people. Chinese people care about the goals of a democratic system, which is primarily concerned with achieving good governance, rather than establishing a multi-party system or universal suffrage.

-- Effective Response to Public Opinions

The Chinese perception of democracy echoes with the viewpoints of some Western scholars. Arend Lijphart believes that a democracy that cannot respond to public opinion is invalid democracy; Giovanni Sartori believes that a good democracy must respond to public opinion, and Robert A. Dahl believes that under an ideal democracy, voters have ultimate control over the political agenda.[1]

In 2020, the Chinese government, for the first time, solicited public opinion and suggestions through the internet

---

[1] Yang Guangbin, Delimiting Democracy, China Renmin University Press, January 2015.

in the formulation of its 14th Five-Year Plan. More than one million suggestions were submitted to the top decision-making officials. Li Dianbo, a college-graduate village official in Inner Mongolia's Dalad Banner region, was surprised that his suggestion on elderly care, submitted online, was adopted by the central authorities.[1]

Under the people-centered development philosophy, the CPC prioritizes issues like food safety, winter heating, air quality, water pollution and housing costs, echoing the top concerns of the public.

As American journalists Theodore H. White and Annalee Jacoby noticed early in 1946, the CPC simply understood that the people wanted change, and it embraced change.[2]

The CPC's promises to the people are announced not in campaign rhetoric but via party policies and resolutions, and the promises must be delivered in practice. "No individual

---

[1] "In-Depth: A netizen's suggestion included in CPC central document", Xinhuanet, Nov. 5, 2020.
http://www.xinhuanet.com/2020-11/05/c_1126703529.htm

[2] Theodore H. White and Annalee Jacoby, Thunder out of China, Xinhua Publishing House, February 1988.

should be left behind in China's battle against poverty," Xi Jinping said during his inspection tour in south China's Guangxi Zhuang Autonomous Region in 2021. "The Chinese people, the CPC, and the CPC leaders always keep their word."[1]

-- Governance-oriented

Political science scholar Yang Guangbin believes that Chinese democracy is a "governance democracy" that seeks good governance. It has three elements - full public participation, autonomous state response, and responsible decision-making and its effective implementation. "Governance democracy" emphasizes not only the democracy of the political process but also the results of democratic politics, or good governance.[2]

China's democracy is centered on governance rather than on elections. The country has maintained long-term

---

[1] Zhang Xiaosong, Zhu Jichai, Du Shangze, Keep Going, Work Hard and Embark on Another Long March -- On-the-Spot Report of CPC General Secretary Xi Jinping's Inspection of Guangxi.
http://www.xinhuanet.com/2021-04/29/c_1127388818.htm
[2] Yang Guangbin, Delimiting Democracy, China Renmin University Press, January 2015.

social stability along with rapid economic growth and has become one of the safest countries in the world. China has set a new goal of modernizing its system of governance to better reflect the will of the people, protect their rights and interests, and inspire their creativity in all its institutions and aspects of governance. This "governance-oriented democracy" will be further strengthened.

3.2 "Efficient Democracy" with Vitality

In a big developing country like China, if there were no enthusiasm, initiative and creativity of the people, there would be no social dynamism; without social dynamism, there would be no great achievements since its reform and opening-up. In a country as complex as China, it would be difficult to imagine the country's current advancements without decision-making authority.

-- Ensembling "Multiple Voices" into "One Piece of Music"

It is observed that China's "democratic centralism" gives the country both dynamism and solid execution. The system gives full play to democracy in order to stimulate the enthusiasm, initiative, and creativity of the people. It also attaches value to proper centralism -- pooling wisdom based on democracy, forming scientific decisions, and putting these into practice. It is the art of combining "multiple voices" into "one piece of music." Thus, the country can effectively prevent decentralism, by which matters are discussed but fail to result in decisions or lead to action.[1]

Democratic centralism is both an organizational principle of the CPC and a principle of state agencies at all levels as stipulated in China's Constitution. It is a principle of decision-making embodied in all aspects of governance and is becoming more procedural and institutionalized.

As affirmed in the provisional regulations on procedures for making major administrative decisions, implemented by China's State Council in 2019, legal reviews and collective discussion are necessary for making major administrative

---

[1] Xi Jinping, Zhejiang, China: A New Vision for Development, Zhejiang People's Publishing House, 2007, P22.

decisions, and executive heads of decision-making organs should make decisions on the basis of collective discussion.

3.3 "Democracy as Driving Force" with Collective Wisdom

China has realized in practice that socialism with Chinese characteristics is a cause for a people surpassing a billion in number. Therefore, the role of the people as the masters of the country must be given full play to ensure the people take the reins of the country. That means democracy is a driving force, that development is meaningful only when it is done for the sake of the people, and development is driven only when it relies on the people.

-- Motivating People Leads to Greatest Democracy

A strong foundation for the success of the CPC is to stick to ensure the principal status of the people and fully mobilize their enthusiasm. Deng Xiaoping has a well-known saying that motivation leads to the greatest democracy. Without democracy, there would be no Chinese miracle. China has expanded its democracy through political, economic, and other reforms and stimulated the enthusiasm, initiative, and creativity of hundreds of millions of people. It has developed productive forces and encouraged the people to participate in reforms and social development. These have become important accelerators that explain the speed of China's modernization since its reform and opening-up.

A typical example is the household responsibility system, originating in Xiaogang Village, Fengyang County, in east China's Anhui Province. On a winter night in 1978, 18 villagers signed a contract with their red fingerprints, dividing the village's collective land into individual households. This initiative gradually spread throughout the country and aroused the enthusiasm of hundreds of millions of farmers, thus launching a new chapter in China's rural reforms. China's reform and opening-up began with the promotion of democracy. A national discussion on the standard of truth adopted the belief that "practice is the sole criterion of truth." Since then, society has become more active than ever, with productive forces continuously unleashed and institutional reforms and innovations becoming the norm.

Convenient Transport Facilitates People's Travel

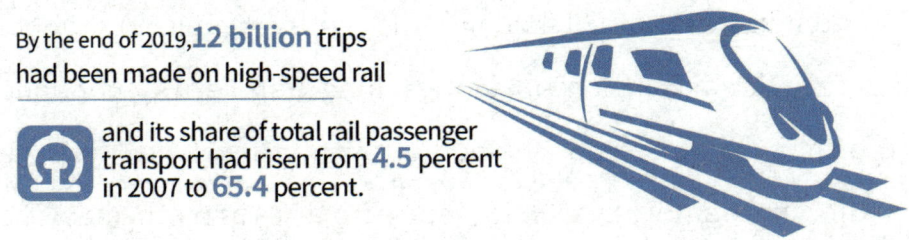

By the end of 2019, **12 billion** trips had been made on high-speed rail

and its share of total rail passenger transport had risen from **4.5** percent in 2007 to **65.4** percent.

Source: Sustainable Development of Transport in China

Creating a Comprehensive Infrastructure Network

By the end of 2019, China had a total of **139,000** km of rail track, of which high-speed lines represented **35,000** km.

China had a total of more than **5 million** km of highways, of which expressways represented **150,000 km**.

Source: Sustainable Development of Transport in China

-- Interaction Between Development and Freedom

China is committed to empowerment through development and "investing in its people" to expand their free development. In parallel, the expansion of freedom brings about the further liberation of productive forces and the increase of human and social capital, helping boost national development.

China's experience shows that development is a process of extending the real freedom enjoyed by people. As Nobel laureate Amartya Sen observes, long before its economic reforms, China was a pioneer in promoting social change in the contemporary world, specifically through massive progress in education, health care, and land reform. He notes China made remarkable progress after the reforms, and that the complementarity between social progress and economic development was well illustrated in China's experience. [1]

-- Dreams Illuminate Reality

Today, China's all-round development and progress has provided a broad space for every Chinese to pursue their dreams. Every Chinese individual's determination to achieve a better life brings together a majestic force to realize the Chinese Dream. The Chinese Dream is an organic combination of individual pursuits and the dream of national rejuvenation as well as the unity of people's comprehensive

---

[1] Development As Freedom, by Amartya Sen (India), China Renmin University Press, 2013, preface of Chinese version.

development and the overall progress of the country. The Chinese Dream offers a new vision for more than 1.4 billion Chinese to pursue democracy, freedom and human rights. It will also inspire the Chinese people to contribute their wisdom and strength.

Over the past 100 years, the CPC has delivered outstanding results for the people of China. Today, the Party is uniting and leading the people on a new road to achieving its second centenary goal. Democracy is a question that must be answered, because "without democracy, there can be no socialism, no socialist modernization, and no great rejuvenation of the Chinese nation."[1]

3.4 Testable "Systematic Democracy"

It is not easy to evaluate whether a political system is democratic or advanced, and the difficulty lies in the lack of objective and comprehensive criteria. China has proposed eight criteria for measuring democracy.

---

[1] Xi Jinping, speech at the celebration of the 60th anniversary of the founding of the National People's Congress, September 5, 2014.

-- The "Eight Whether or Not" Criteria on Democracy[1]

Column: The "Eight Whether or Not" Criteria on Democracy

Whether the succession of its leaders is conducted in an orderly way in accordance with the law;

Whether government affairs and social, economic and cultural affairs are managed by all the people in accordance with the law;

Whether the public freely voices its demands to advance its interests;

Whether all stakeholders in society are fully involved in the country's political process;

Whether government decisions are made in a sound and democratic way;

Whether outstanding individuals in all sectors can enter government leadership teams and the governance system through fair competition;

Whether the governing party exercises leadership over government affairs in accordance with the Constitution and the law;

Whether the exercise of power is kept under effective checks and supervision.

---

[1] Xi Jinping, speech at the celebration of the 60th anniversary of the founding of the National People's Congress, September 5, 2014.

Chapter III A Democracy that Works: a Touchstone for Testing Institutional Effectiveness

Political scholars maintain that the "Eight Whether or Not" criteria summarize lessons learned from the development of democratic politics at home and abroad, conform to the principles of modern political civilization, and reflect the systematic nature of the whole process of people's democracy. From a global perspective, this is a theoretical exploration deeply rooted in reality. [1]

A comprehensive view of democracy. The criteria for judging whether a political system is democratic and its degree of democracy should not be one-sided but comprehensive and holistic.

A developmental view of democracy. Democracy is a process of continuous development and evolution, constantly evolving from low to high, from tradition to modern, and the building of democracy is a work in progress.

A result-oriented view of democracy. Effective democracy combines formal democracy and substantive

---

[1] Zheng Changzhong, director of the research center for political party building and national development, Fudan University, in an interview with Xinhua News Agency in September 2021.

democracy, indirect democracy and direct democracy, and objectively evaluates the political system based on actual results.

According to studies by the Ash Center for Democratic Governance and Innovation at Harvard University's John F. Kennedy School of Government, the Chinese people's degree of trust in the Communist Party of China has exceeded 90 percent for more than 10 years in a row.[1]

According to a survey conducted by York University in Canada, 98 percent of the Chinese public is satisfied with the central government; for local governments, satisfaction exceeds 90 percent.[2]

Some international observers have concluded that few in the West have realized that the Communist Party of China has provided the best governance in China's history. The essence of democracy means government by the people,

---

[1] Edward Cunningham, Tony Saich & Jesse Turiel, Understanding CCP Resilience: Surveying Chinese Public Opinion Through Time, Harvard Kennedy School Ash Center, July 2020.

[2] U.S. Media: Poll shows Chinese people's trust in government is up to 98 percent, Reference News' website, May 8, 2021, original English version from The Washington Post's website, May 5, 2021.

said former Singaporean foreign minister George Yeo. "And by that definition, China is a democracy."[1]

---

[1] Former Singaporean Foreign Minister George Yong-boon Yeo in an Exclusive Interview with Global Times: China Has Its Own Way of Realizing Democracy, Global Times, June 8, 2021. https://world.huanqiu.com/article/43RmktCXG2J

Chapter IV

The Wisdom of Practice: The Enlightenment of Pursuing Common Values of Humanity

The right approach is to act on the vision of a community with a shared future for mankind. We should uphold the common values of humanity, i.e., peace, development, equity, justice, democracy and freedom, rise above ideological prejudice, make the mechanisms, principles and policies of our cooperation as open and inclusive as possible, and jointly safeguard world peace and stability.[1]

— Xi Jinping

---

[1] Special address by Chinese President Xi Jinping at the World Economic Forum Virtual Event of the Davos Agenda, Jan. 25, 2021.

Chapter IV The Wisdom of Practice: The Enlightenment of Pursuing Common Values of Humanity

The common values of humanity are the natural results of the interconnection and interaction of human beings in the long-term process of socialization, and also the natural outcomes of the evolution of human history from the nation to the world. These values are the wealth of human civilization, the key to solving the problems of our time, and the greatest common denominator in building a better world.

Under the leadership of the CPC, the Chinese people have carried out a large-scale democratic practice from scratch and unremittingly pursued freedom and human rights, not only for the happiness of the Chinese people and the rejuvenation of the Chinese nation, but also for the progress of humankind and the common prosperity of the world. China has created more opportunities for the world by promoting its own development, and explored the laws of human social development by deepening its own practices.

China's experience shows that democracy, freedom and human rights are interconnected, interdependent and mutually reinforcing. A good democracy is a guarantee of freedom and human rights, and people with freedom and human rights are a dynamic force for democracy and progress. Among the three, democracy can be implemented as the carrier of institutions. By enhancing the linchpin of democratic construction, people's freedom and rights will have institutional guarantees.

If pursuing the common values of humanity means "doing the right thing," then "doing the right thing right" is a great practical challenge. China's path of democracy, freedom and human rights has provided useful insights.

4.1 Approach to Sound Governance: Three Leading Features

China's pursuit of democracy, freedom and human rights is carried out in two contexts: one is China's pursuit of modernization and the other is the sweeping trend of globalization. Dani Rodrik, a professor at Harvard, once put forward the well-known globalization trilemma: "We cannot have hyperglobalization, democracy, and national self-determination all at once."[1] The reality in China proves this

---

[1] (Britain) Edward Luce, The Retreat of Western Liberalism, Shanxi People's Publishing House, February 2019, 1st edition, P70.

assertion wrong. Over the past few decades, China has been an enthusiastic participant in globalization, adhered to the path of independent development, and creatively developed socialist democracy with Chinese characteristics. This shows China's strong capacity for governance. A growing number of political scientists, including Francis Fukuyama who put forward "The end of history" idea, recognize the critical importance of national governance in global governance in the 21st century.

The practice of democracy, freedom and human rights in China has helped develop a series of effective governance ideas and methods. An advanced non-partisan party, a people-centered philosophy, and a development-focused worldview can probably be described as the three "leading features" of China's approach to sound governance.

Feature 1: Advanced Non-partisan Party

To understand today's China, one must understand the CPC. "Upholding the centralized and unified leadership of the CPC, adhering to the Party's scientific theory, ensuring political stability, and ensuring that the country always moves in the direction of socialism."[1] This ranks first among the remarkable advantages of China's state system and its governance system.

The CPC is a political party in a special sense. It represents the fundamental interests of the overwhelming majority of the people and does not represent the interests of any interest group, any powerful group, or any privileged class. Its governance focuses on the long-term stability of the country, not on short-term election campaigns. As a prominent feature of an advanced political party, the CPC has always acted in the interests of the people, followed the trend of the progress of humankind and the times, taken charge of the overall situation, coordinated with all parties, united and organized all political forces and resources, and striven for the happiness of all the people and the rejuvenation for the Chinese nation. It has its own logic of action.

---

[1] The Communist Party of China Central Committee's decision on some major issues concerning how to uphold and improve the system of socialism with Chinese characteristics and advance the modernization of China's system and capacity for governance, adopted by the fourth plenary session of the 19th CPC Central Committee, on Oct.31, 2019.

Unlike the so-called "one-party dictatorship" misinterpreted by the outside world, China's new political party system can be perceived as a democratic practice of "1+8+N." Except for the CPC, there are eight non-CPC political parties in China. Despite being small in number, these parties consist of influential people, with a majority of them being intellectuals. Their participation in political affairs has provided an indispensable contribution of knowledge for the governing party's decision-making process. In addition to the CPC and eight non-CPC political parties, there are also those without any party affiliation and members of the general public, who can also participate in the country's democratic agenda through a variety of means.

One-party leadership has ensured the authority of governance, the efficiency of democratic decision-making and the continuity of policies, while consultation by multiple parties has enabled the CPC to pool its wisdom from a wide spectrum of talent. The contribution by people as a whole has enabled those charged with the governance of the country to unite the greatest number of people. The combination of democracy and centralization has effectively reduced the internal consumption of political resources. Intra-party oversight and constantly developing social oversight have ensured democratic accountability both inside and outside the Party.

The CPC has endured an arduous struggle for the Chinese people to enjoy democracy, freedom and human rights, and created one miracle after another for the people's well-being. The CPC is highly conscious, disciplined and self-sacrificing. It can truly represent and unite the people and has sufficient authority. The leadership of the CPC is crucial to the governance of such a large country like China. As Deng Xiaoping, the chief architect of China's reform and opening up, said, "...without the unified leadership of such a party, it would be unimaginable, and the country would only be divided and accomplish nothing."[1]

Feature 2: People-centered Philosophy

"A country would collapse without the support of its people." Confucius had pointed out the key criteria for good

---

[1] Selected Works of Deng Xiaoping, Volume II, People's Publishing House, 1994, P341-342.

government more than 2,000 years ago. Public support is the people's trust in those charged with the governance. Only when the "people-centered" approach is taken as the starting point of policy-decision can the effectiveness of politics be trusted by the people. It is a credo of the governing party in China that people's support is the highest political priority.

Today, about one out of 10 adult Chinese is a member of the CPC. They are everywhere. The Party's goal is to serve the people wholeheartedly; its original aspiration and founding mission is to seek happiness for the people and rejuvenation for the nation, and putting the people first is enshrined in its values. The flesh-and-blood ties between the Party and the people signify both the source and destination of power.

The "people-centered" philosophy has endowed China's politics and governance with solid value. In the governance of modern Chinese society, "service" has become a keyword, "people's satisfaction" has become a new yardstick of political achievements, and the government and the society are forming a new kind of contract.

Increasing Average Life Expectancy of Chinese Population

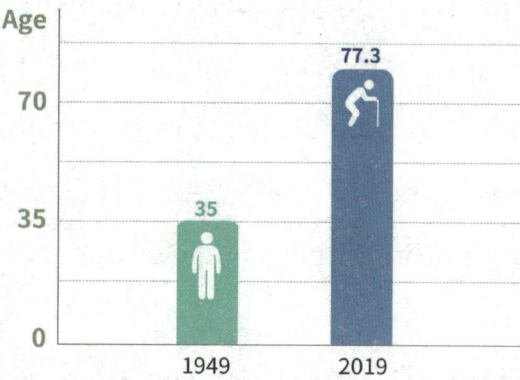

In 2019, the life expectancy of Chinese citizens rose to **77.3** years, compared with **35** years in 1949

Source: The Communist Party of China and Human Rights Protection – A 100-Year Quest

China's Improving Living Conditions and Healthcare

 At the start of reform and opening up the per capita floor space of urban residents was only **6.7** square meters and rural residents **8.1** square meters. In 2019, the corresponding figures were **39.8** square meters and **48.9** square meters.

 In 2020, the basic medical insurance scheme covered **1.36 billion** people.

 In 2018, the number of health service institutions in China increased to **997,000**, a **271.78**-fold increase from 1949.

 All poor populations have access to **basic medical insurance, serious illness insurance, and medical assistance**. Basic medical insurance coverage of the poor remains almost 100 percent.

Sources: Seeking Happiness for People: The Communist Party of China and Human Rights Protection– A 100-Year Quest, 70 Years of Progress on Human Rights in China, Moderate Prosperity in All Respects: Another Milestone Achieved in China's Human Rights

Chinese People's Enrollment Rate, Illiteracy and Higher Education Rate

In the early days of the People's Republic of China, China's education system was poor and the general level of education was low.
The net primary education enrollment rate was **20** percent and the gross junior secondary education enrollment rate was only **3** percent.
There were only **117,000** college students and **80** percent of the population was illiterate.

The gross enrollment rate in senior secondary education increased from **42.8** percent in 2000 to **91.2** percent in 2020.

The gross enrollment rate in higher education rose from **12.5** percent in 2000 to **54.4** percent in 2020. China has built the world's largest higher education system, with over 40 million students on campus.

Sources: 70 Years of Progress on Human Rights in China, Moderate Prosperity in All Respects: Another Milestone Achieved in China's Human Rights

--"Governance Quotient"

In China, the fundamental criterion for judging the success or failure of any work is whether the people support it or not. If such criterion was applied to judge the efficiency of governance, it can be seen that Chinese society is characterized by a high degree of "governance quotient." In short, these characteristics refer to people's sense of security, gain and happiness. Corresponding to the "three senses," it is the government's abilities to secure stable, prosperous and happy lives for the people. The continuous progress of China's practices of democracy, freedom and human rights, an irrefutable fact, shows that the value of people-centered governance philosophy is by no means a political slogan.

Feature 3: Development-focused Worldview

China's outlook on the world focuses on development, noted a March 2020 report by RAND Corporation. Such a worldview will probably give China a unique advantage when competing with other countries in the 21st century.

For more than 70 years, the Party and the government have focused on development, enabling the Chinese people to gain more and more freedom and democratic rights. In turn, more freedom and democratic rights have further promoted the development of the whole country. The outcomes of development continue to help improve democratic governance so that the rights of the people are better protected. The dialectics of development and freedom, and the interaction between democracy and human rights, are vividly reflected in China's practices. Such ideas of development in China, through globalization, have been transmitted to the rest of the world, enhancing global well-being.

By firmly upholding multilateralism, fairness and justice, and upholding the goals and principles of the UN Charter, China has played an important stabilizing role and brought certainty, confidence and hope to the world, according to UN Secretary-General Antonio Guterres. He

Chapter IV The Wisdom of Practice: The Enlightenment of Pursuing Common Values of Humanity

maintains that history will prove that China's development is not only an irresistible historical trend but also a major contribution to the progress of human civilization.

Changes in Urban and Rural Incomes in China

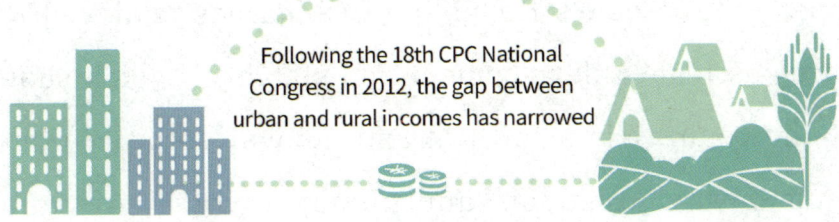

Following the 18th CPC National Congress in 2012, the gap between urban and rural incomes has narrowed with the ratio of disposable income falling to **2.69** in 2018.

Source: Seeking Happiness for People: 70 Years of Progress on Human Rights in China

Changes in Ratio of Urban and Rural income

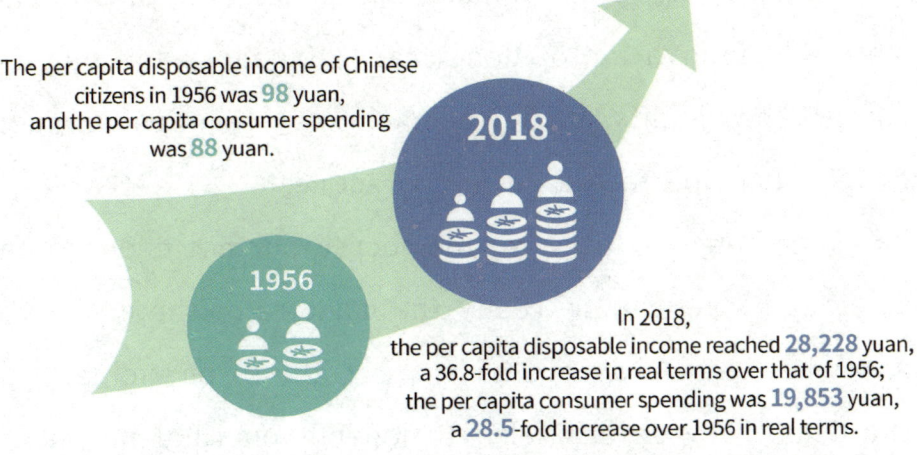

The per capita disposable income of Chinese citizens in 1956 was **98** yuan, and the per capita consumer spending was **88** yuan.

In 2018, the per capita disposable income reached **28,228** yuan, a 36.8-fold increase in real terms over that of 1956; the per capita consumer spending was **19,853** yuan, a **28.5**-fold increase over 1956 in real terms.

Source: Seeking Happiness for People: 70 Years of Progress on Human Rights in China

4.2 Realizing the Common Values of Humanity: "Four Principles"

Through adhering to the common values and ideals of humanity and seeking to achieve them in a down-to-earth manner, the People's Republic of China has achieved the miraculous feat in development and stability, which shows that the country is a faithful and innovative practitioner of democracy, freedom and human rights, providing inspiration for realizing the common values of humanity.

Result-oriented

"Theory, dear friend, is gray, but the golden tree of life springs evergreen." Abundant practice is the theoretical source of innovation of democracy, freedom and human rights. The validity of the theory and system design must be tested and perfected through practice.

Whether a country is a democracy or not depends on whether its people are really the masters of the country, and whether the people have the right to participate in the democracy extensively; It depends on what promises are made during the election process, and even more on how many of these promises are fulfilled after the election; It depends on what political procedures and rules are stipulated by the system and laws, and whether such systems and laws are really implemented; It depends on whether the rules and procedures for the exercise of power are democratic, and more importantly, whether power is truly supervised and restricted by the people.[1]

China's democratic practice is characterized by "the people are the masters of the country," a "whole-process people's democracy," the eight "whether or nots," and "going one's own way," creating a new form of political culture.

Self-determination

Democracy is the right of all peoples, not an exclusive right of a few people or countries. Whether a country is democratic, whether its people are free and whether their human rights are guaranteed should be judged by the people of the country or the international community,

---

[1] Xi Jinping's remarks at a central conference on work related to people's congresses held in Beijing, Oct. 14, 2021.

not by a few outsiders nor a small group of self-righteous countries. People of all countries have the right to choose their own development path and system. This is essential for people's happiness and conforms to the spirit of democracy. To impose one's own view of democracy, freedom and human rights on others is a violation of the true spirit of democracy, freedom and human rights. The development of the current international situation has proved China's view that external military intervention and so-called "democratic transformation" only cause endless harm.

To develop democracy, all countries must walk out of the mist of dogmatism and discourse hegemony and explore their own way independently. Successful democratic constructions have their own characteristics. The diversity of democratic formation, organization and operation is the root of the vitality and creativity of modern political civilization. China's democracy must be deeply rooted in Chinese society, rather than copied from foreign countries. It could ruin a country's future if it merely copies the political systems of other countries.

Steady-paced

The realization of democracy and freedom and the development of human rights have prerequisites, sequences and foundations. Based on their national conditions, different countries need to make gradual progress, neither losing any opportunity nor skipping any stage of development. A country should formulate a roadmap and timetable for action by taking into account various factors including the intensity of reform, the speed of development and the tolerable level of society. For those countries that imported foreign democratic models and failed in their development, an important reason for their failure is that they did not coordinate the relationship between development and timing and sequence according to their own reality, which has led to a series of problems such as social disorder, political turmoil and repeated setbacks in economic and social development.

Chinese People's Employment

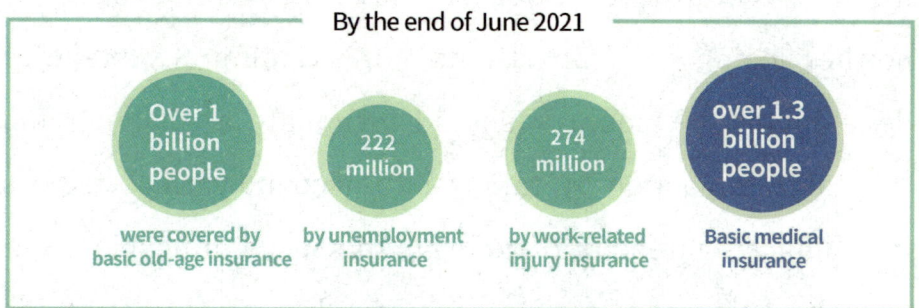

At the end of 2020, almost **751 million** people in China were in employment.
China has built the world's **largest social security network**.

By the end of June 2021

- Over 1 billion people were covered by basic old-age insurance
- 222 million by unemployment insurance
- 274 million by work-related injury insurance
- over 1.3 billion people Basic medical insurance

Source: The CPC: Its Mission and Contributions

Column: China's View of Human Rights in the New Era

"People's happy lives are the greatest human right" is China's view of human rights in the new era. The fourth national human rights action plan (2021-2025) sets out a new agenda, which requires the country to take a people-centered development thought and take promoting well-rounded human development and common prosperity as the purpose of human rights; to develop a whole-process people's democracy, safeguard social fairness and justice, focus on solving people's urgent problems and worries, ensure that all people's human rights are guaranteed at a higher level, and to continuously enhance people's sense of acquisition, happiness and security for human rights protection.

China's human rights development, prioritizing the basic rights of subsistence and development, keeps gaining momentum in its content and standards, moving towards the goal that living a life of contentment is the ultimate human right.

Ever-progressing

The pursuit of democracy and freedom as well as respect for and protection of human rights is an endless process of improvement. The democratic practice of the West started the process of modern democracy, but it does not mean that the development of democracy will end in the Western model. The realization of democracy, freedom and human rights must follow the development of practice and must be localized to take root. The exploration of people of different countries will enrich and improve the practice of democracy, freedom and human rights of humanity, and make the common values of humanity more vivid, instead of being gradually hollowed out.

> **Column: China's View of Freedom**
>
> In practice, China has continuously liberated and developed productive forces, forming a Chinese concept of freedom with "all-around development of humans" as its connotation. The Chinese concept of freedom endows people with great material and spiritual freedom, promotes the free and all-round development of people, coordinates the relations between fairness and efficiency, order and vitality, power and rights in practice, and realizes the dialectical unity of common ideals and individual pursuit, collectivism and individual development, collective will and individual freedom.

4.3 "Questions of the Times": China's Solution

"What has happened to the world and how should we respond?" Chinese President Xi Jinping asked the fundamental questions of the times at the United Nations Office in Geneva on Jan. 18, 2017.

Under the impact of the COVID-19 pandemic and at a juncture of great historical changes, how can civilization develop and how can human beings coexist? Xi threw new light on these questions while addressing a commemorative meeting marking the 50th anniversary of the restoration of the People's Republic of China's lawful seat at the United Nations on Oct. 25, 2021. "We should vigorously advocate peace, development, equity, justice, democracy and freedom, which are the common values of humanity, and work together to provide the right guiding philosophy for building a better world," Xi said. "Peace and development are our common cause, equity and justice our common aspiration, and democracy and freedom our common pursuit."

-- Return to Common Sense

The world today is witnessing the deterioration of democracy and a distorted perspective of freedom and human rights. Governance in some countries is quite concerning. "The poverty of democracy" is an indisputable fact featuring various crises such as polarized politics, polarization between the rich and the poor, failure of governance and bullying by other countries. It is also manifested by the fact that the theory of "liberal democracy" cannot explain reality, let alone solve problems. This perfectly describes a "paradigm crisis" outlined by scholars -- human beings need a new framework and new knowledge to break through the current predicament to realize the common values of humanity in an era of globalization.

Democracy does not equal good governance, and may even cause turmoil. The real crisis is thought-provoking. If we want to "strengthen" and "update" democracy, we must return to "common sense" and ask, what is democracy? As China's practice shows, the true meaning of democracy holds people as the masters of the country. True democracy also stands for equality and justice, good governance and people's well-being. In international relations, it means that "the internal affairs of a country should be handled by the country's own people, and international affairs should be managed by all countries through consultation."[1]

The knowledge gained by more than 1.4 billion Chinese people down their arduous path to democracy, freedom and human rights deserves due recognition. China's approach to democracy, freedom, human rights has boosted confidence in, deepened understanding of and offered a solution for

---

[1] "Xi attends a joint summit of the leaders of the Shanghai Cooperation Organization (SCO) and the Collective Security Treaty Organization (CSTO) member states on the Afghanistan issue," www.xinhuanet.com, Sept. 17, 2021. http://www.news.cn/politics/leaders/2021-09/17/c_1127874704.htm

solving challenges to democracy, freedom and human rights and the governance deficit facing humankind.

-- Diversity: Rational and Desirable

Peace, development, equity, justice, democracy and freedom are the common values of humanity, but the paths to realization are personalized. We should respect the explorations of different peoples to turn their values into reality. By doing so, the common values of humanity will be translated into the practice of individual countries to serve the interests of their own people in a concrete and realistic way. The acts of those who believe their civilization is superior and insist on transforming or replacing other civilizations with a given model are just absurd and arbitrary and will result in catastrophe. There are enough lessons to be learned.

The diversity of human civilization makes the world vivid. Diversity brings communication, communication breeds integration, and integration produces progress. Diversity not only makes sense but also is desirable. One should value not only one's own culture but also contribute to the flourishing of all cultures. Countries should communicate with and learn from each other to jointly drive the progress of human civilizations amid the harmonious and diversified practices of democratic politics and human rights. The significance of being guided by the common values of humanity is rammed home in the motto of the 2022 Beijing Olympic and Paralympic Winter Games -- "Together for a Shared Future."

-- A Community with a Shared Future for Mankind

It was once believed that the country is the largest political unit and the world is just an empty geographical space. The truth today is that human beings are a whole, and the planet they live in is a "global village," where no country can isolate itself from the rest of the world. Global multipolarity and democratization of international relations are the general trends seen today. Only by seizing the historical opportunity and making correct choices can humankind create a brighter future. From the ancient Chinese philosophy of "a just cause should be pursued for common good" to "a community with a shared future for mankind," the Chinese concept of "the whole world is one family" chalks out the right direction for the world wandering at a crossroads.

Chapter IV The Wisdom of Practice: The Enlightenment of Pursuing Common Values of Humanity

Democracy and freedom are the core elements of the common values of humanity, and human rights are the ideals for which people of all countries strive unremittingly. In the socialist practice of defending democracy, freedom and human rights, the Communist Party of China (CPC) has put people's overall interests on top of the agenda in its political endeavors, maintained the logic of giving democracy back to the people, and advocated the principles that freedom should enhance the all-round development of the people, and happiness is the ultimate standard of human rights. The CPC has pioneered a new path to China's modernization, and created a new model for human civilization, thus offering Chinese solutions of world significance as answers to the questions of our times.

Conclusion

Humanity's common values of peace, development, equity, justice, democracy, and freedom are the basis for building a community with a shared future for mankind. As the saying goes that "all roads lead to Rome," to achieve that end, it is necessary for all countries to constantly explore the best path that is most suitable for the interests of their people according to their own national conditions.

In exchanges with the world, China has found a path of modernization with Chinese characteristics, which has proved effective in practice. As Chinese leader Xi Jinping pointed out: "The great social transformation of contemporary China is not a master copy of China's history and culture, nor a copy of the template envisaged by classical Marxist writers. It is also not a copy of the socialist practice of other countries, nor a copy of the modernization of foreign countries."

China continues to make progress in promoting democracy, safeguarding freedom, and protecting human rights, but the road ahead is still full of challenges. More than 1.4 billion people are moving towards common prosperity both materially and spiritually. China still needs to continuously promote the modernization of its political system and capacity for governance, constantly strengthen exchanges and mutual learning with other countries, and work together to advance the cause of human progress.

There is no end to exploration and pursuit.

Editor's Note and Acknowledgments

"Pursuing Common Values of Humanity -- China's Approach to Democracy, Freedom and Human Rights" was written by a research team headed by He Ping, president of the Xinhua News Agency and director of the academic board of New China Research, a think tank under Xinhua. Fu Hua, editor-in-chief of Xinhua, served as deputy head of the team, and Zhang Sutang, vice president of Xinhua, served as project director. Team members included Sun Chengbin, Liu Gang, Ban Wei, Chu Guoqiang, Gu Qianjiang, Liu Lina, Cui Feng, Ye Shuhong, Hao Weiwei, Liu Yang, Xuan Liqi, Zong Wei, Li Huaiyan, Liang Jianqiang, Chen Shangying, Zhou Rui, Yan Rui, Liu

Mingxia, among others.

During the writing of the report, extensive assistance and guidance were received from Zhao Qizheng, former director of the State Council Information Office; Li Junru, former deputy head of the Party School of the CPC Central Committee; Zhang Baijia, former deputy director of the Party History Research Center of the CPC Central Committee; Lu Guangjin, secretary-general of the China Society for Human Rights Studies; Yang Guangbin, dean of the School of International Studies of Renmin University of China (RUC); Zhu Liyu, professor at Law School at RUC; Zhang Fei'an, associate professor at the School of Marxism Studies at RUC; Diao Daming, associate professor at the National Academy of Development and Strategy at RUC; Zhang Shuhua, head of the Institute of Political Science (IPS) at the Chinese Academy of Social Sciences (CASS); Fan Peng, director of the Research Center of Contemporary Chinese Politics of IPS, CASS; Xu Bu, president of China Institute of International Studies(CIIS); Gao Fei, vice president of China Foreign Affairs University; Wang Huiyao, president of the Center for China and Globalization; Tang Shiqi, dean of the

School of International Studies of Peking University; Xu Jianwei, professor at the China Studies Institute of Peking University; Chen Lai, dean of the Tsinghua Academy of Chinese Learning; Yan Yilong, deputy dean of the Institute for Contemporary China Studies of Tsinghua University; Tang Shiping, Chen Zhouwang and Han Fuguo, professors at the School of International Relations & Public Affairs of Fudan University; Zheng Changzhong, associate professor at the School of International Relations & Public Affairs of Fudan University; Ma Zhongfa, professor at Fudan University Law School; Lu Zhi'an, associate professor at Fudan University Law School; Chen Yun, professor at the Department of Philosophy of East China Normal University (ECNU); Liu Jun, deputy dean of the School of politics and international studies at ECNU; Yan Dexue, associate researcher of the School pf politics and international studies at ECNU; Ouyang Kang, director of the Institute of State Governance of Huazhong University of Science and Technology (HUST); Wang Xigen, head of the Institute for Human Rights Law at HUST; Yue Kui, dean of the School of Marxism at HUST; Zhang Mingxin, dean of the Journalism and Information Communication School at HUST; Daniel A. Bell, dean of the School of Political Science and Public Administration of Shandong University; Kong Xinfeng, deputy head of the Institute of State Governance of Shandong University; Altantsan, Party chief of Inner Mongolia Normal University; He Zhipeng, executive director of Jilin University Human Rights Center; Meng Qingtao, deputy dean of the Institute of Human Rights at Southwest University of Political Science & Law; Song Lidan and Meng Qingyou, associate research fellows at the Academy of Marxism, CASS.

Errors or omissions might appear in this report due to inadequate information and the limited knowledge of the authors. Your comments and criticism are welcome.